...isms

...isms

UNDERSTANDING FASHION

MAIRI MACKENZIE

UNIVERSE

Contents

Fashion holds a mirror up to the societies within which it exists. It operates as both a cultural phenomenon and a highly complex business and as such it reflects the social, economic, sexual and political attitudes of an era.

Distinct from ceremonial and national dress, fashion is characterised by unceasing, unrelenting change. It is always moving on, driven not by necessity but by a highly complex and deeply entrenched system in which social distinction, sartorial novelty and economic considerations compel change. However, this is not to say that fashion is simply a frivolity encouraged by a morally bankrupt economic system and indulged in by the vain. Nor can it be said that fashion impacts only upon those who choose to participate in it.

The study of fashion is inclusive. It is not limited to the rarefied world of Haute Couture, designer labels, glossy magazines and the social elite. The complex economic, political and cultural issues associated with the production and consumption of fashion impact upon all sectors of society. Advances in the production of fashion have been a catalyst for the mass industrialisation, urbanisation and globalisation that have defined the modern era. Also, fashion is integral to the construction and communication of one's social identity, helping to delineate the class, sexuality, age, ethnicity and particularly the gender of the wearer, as well as being expressive of an individual's cultural preferences. Indeed, developments in fashion and the often extreme public reaction to them have highlighted and helped to address (if not resolve) deep-rooted social prejudices felt by women, gay and lesbian communities, the young, various ethnic minorities and the working classes.

This book is an introductory guide to the major 'isms' that have shaped fashion history from the 17th century to the present day. It is intended to provide a straightforward and easy to understand guide that identifies the context, evolution, key characteristics and significance of each ism. Limited space precludes a full analysis of the breadth and depth of each subject; instead the reader should use this as a stepping-off point for further avenues of enquiry. Also, owing to the enormity of the subject, many moments in fashion history have been necessarily excluded.

The choice of the 17th century as a starting point reflects not the date from whence fashion originated, but the availability of surviving costume and the point at which changes in fashion began to gather momentum.

Unless otherwise specified, all mention of fashion refers to clothing worn in the economically developed countries of the Western world. On many occasions isms overlap, occurring simultaneously or exhibiting shared characteristics and key participants. Although the division of the book into four main sections according to century is something of an artificially imposed classification system, it provides the reader with an easy to negotiate structure.

How to use this book

Symbols are used to distinguish between the three types of ism outlined in this introduction. This means you can tell at a glance whether an ism is a broad cultural trend **BCT**, a trend within fashion **TWF** or one that has been given an appropriate moniker by the author where one did not previously exist and is therefore an author-defined trend **ADT**.

A BROAD CULTURAL TREND
e.g. Romanticism, Modernism
An ism where trends that are apparent in other areas of culture (such as literature, music, the fine arts and decorative arts) are simultaneously evident within fashion. These are the most wide-ranging of all the isms and within them a number of more localised or specific isms might be apparent.

TWF **A TREND WITHIN FASHION**
e.g. Dandyism, The New Look
These isms are specific to fashion and refer to a particular moment or a definable group of people working within, or expressive of, the trend.

ADT **AUTHOR-DEFINED TREND**
These are isms that, although they are integral to an understanding of fashion, do not already have an appropriate moniker. These terms are specific to this book and provide a succinct and relevant means of categorising the ism.

INTRODUCTION
The first section offers a brief introduction to the ism and provides a succinct summary of its main features.

Celebrity Consumerism **BCT**

Celebrities are the sartorial bellwethers of the Postmodern age. Traditional hierarchies whereby the masses sought to emulate the fashions created and worn by the upper classes have broken down and instead our aspirations are fixed on the figure of the celebrity.

CATHY McGOWAN (1943–); GIANNI VERSACE (1946–97); ELIZABETH HURLEY (1965–); SARAH JESSICA PARKER (1965–); ASHLEY OLSEN (1986–); MARY-KATE OLSEN (1986–)

Postmodern; emulation; aspiration; age of celebrity; coolspotters; endorsement

We are, it is said, living in an age of celebrity, in which there is a heightened fascination with and unquenchable appetite for information on where they go, what they do and who they do it with. Analogous to this has been the effect of the celebrity upon our consumption patterns, most obviously expressed in the contemporary obsession with celebrity fashion.

A commercial framework has been constructed to capitalise on this fascination with the style of the celebrity. On the Internet, sites like As Seen On Screen (asos.com) specialise in selling replica and original versions of clothing worn by celebrities, and coolspotters (coolspotters.com), although not a direct retail site, provides a one-stop portal to identifying the products, brands and fashions worn by particular celebrities and their fictional alter egos. Magazines wholly devoted to celebrity fashion provide commentary on their style and offer step-by-step guides to getting the look, and the letters pages are filled with requests as to where one can go to purchase celebrity-endorsed items. Designers, aware of the influence of celebrity upon their own profiles, strategically ally themselves with those who are representative of the image they wish to project. Celebrities have not restricted their endorsement of products to associating with, starring in the advertisements for or wearing the clothing of a particular designer, and (not letting a lack of fashion training get in the way of a good money spinner) many famous faces have now put their weight behind their own-name celebrity brands. Some are known for their sense of style and use their sartorial credibility to carry them through; ranges like Sarah Jessica Parker's 'Bitten' for US

budget retailer Steve and Barry's and 'The Row' by Olsen twins Ashley and Mary-Kate do not stretch the credulity of the consumer. Others, although perhaps well dressed, have no more than a spurious association with fashion: 'Sweetface' by Jennifer Lopez and 'Mblem' by Mandy Moore being a case in point.

Although we are experiencing a heightened version of Celebrity Consumerism, this phenomenon is not, however, exclusive to the 21st century. Hollywood and its stars in the 1930s exerted a huge influence upon contemporary fashions. The studios thus promoted copies of popular outfits and magazines dedicated to replicating the styles onscreen became popular. In the 1960s the outfits worn by Cathy McGowan, presenter of British music show 'Ready Steady Go!', were copied slavishly by young women encouraging McGowan to launch a celebrity-endorsed clothing range.

◄ Gianni Versace, Evening dresses, 1996
◄ and Spring/Summer 1991. The Costume Institute, Metropolitan Museum of Art, New York, US
It could reasonably be argued that Gianni Versace, having recognised the glamour, excitement and commercial pull that surrounded them, was a key catalyst in the contemporary veneration of celebrities within the fashion industry. He filled the front row of his shows with celebrity faces, and on the catwalk always used celebrity supermodels. His overtly sexy outfits have been worn by and made the careers of numerous celebrities (most notably Elizabeth Hurley who wore a headline-grabbing safety-pinned Versace dress to the premiere of her boyfriend Hugh Grant's movie), and the adverts have featured the faces of celebrity icons including Madonna, Courtney Love, Halle Berry and Britney Spears. The example on the right was designed for US singing superstar Tina Turner.

OTHER COLLECTIONS
AUSTRALIA Powerhouse Museum, Sydney
ENGLAND Fashion Museum, Bath; Gallery of Costume, Platt Hall, Manchester; Victoria and Albert Museum, London
ITALY Galleria del Costume, Palazzo Pitti, Florence
US Chicago History Museum, Chicago, Illinois

Hollywoodism; Postmodernism; Brand Revivalism

Bloomerism; Utility; Japanese Avant-Gardeism

Celebrity Consumerism

KEY FIGURES
This is a list of prominent individuals associated with the ism. This might include, but is not restricted to, designers, innovators, fashion icons and key commentators.

KEY WORDS
These words sum up the key concepts, styles or issues relating to the ism. A contextual understanding of these will help you to quickly chart an ism and enable easier recollection of it.

MAIN DEFINITION
This explores the ism in more depth than the introduction, explaining its significance and history as well the ideas and characteristics that distinguish it from, or relate it to, other isms.

KEY EXAMPLES
Each ism is illustrated with one or two key examples that have been chosen because they best exemplify the features of the ism. All have been selected from publicly accessible museum collections. However, due to the fragile nature of clothing and the need for museums to rotate their permanent exhibitions, you are advised to confirm public access before visiting.

SEE ALSO
Isms are often interrelated. Those listed in this section share an affinity, idea or method with the ism under discussion.

DON'T SEE
Isms are also antithetical to each other, or predicated on mutually exclusive and incompatible assumptions, methods or ideas. The isms listed under Don't See are in some way out of tune with the ism that has just been discussed.

Other resources included in this book

GLOSSARY OF NAMES
All the fashion designers, innovators, arbiters and icons already identified as Key Figures are gathered in an alphabetical list for ease of reference. Other names, although not included within the main body of the book, have been inserted to identify their contribution to fashion. The Glossary of Names also includes, where known, dates of birth and death as well as the ism or isms with which they are most closely identified.

GLOSSARY OF USEFUL TERMS
This contains terms that have been used in definitions of isms as well as a general selection of terms that you might come across as you explore the subject further.

CHRONOLOGY OF ISMS
This time line shows the lifespan of the isms covered in the book. Isms which are broad cultural trends, or trends within fashion, tend to be longer than those defined by designers, critics or historians. Some debate exists as to the start of many isms, while many continue without a discernible end point. The dates chosen to represent these represent an approximation of such debate.

PLACES TO VISIT
This details museums where examples of fashionable dress are held in the permanent collections. However, due to the fragile nature of clothing and the need for museums to rotate their permanent exhibitions, you are advised to confirm public access before visiting.

I

17TH + 18TH
CENTURIES

The fine and decorative arts of the 17th and 18th centuries were dominated first by the Baroque and then the Rococo movement. These broad cultural trends exerted a pervasive stylistic influence upon the architecture, painting, sculpture, music, interior design, textiles and clothing of each period.

Louis XIV; Louis XV; Exoticism; mechanised textile industry; *marchandes de modes*; Anglomania; French Revolution

Baroque fashion was stiff, ornate and formal and the textiles were weighty and exhibited the curvilinear designs typical of the decorative arts in this period. The reign of Louis XIV of France (1667–1715) dominated the era and his sartorial choices set the fashions. He indulged his taste for excessively lavish clothing and interiors, encouraged his court to emulate his extravagance (many of whom were bankrupted in the process) and thus earned himself the moniker of 'the consumer king'.

Rococo fashion was altogether more whimsical. The silhouettes did not deviate dramatically from those worn during the Baroque period, but the decorative detail was distinctly more subtle and the ornamentation more delicate. Just as Baroque reflected the temperament of Louis XIV, so Rococo expressed the disposition of his successor, Louis XV.

Within these broad cultural trends a number of other localised and more transient fashions were apparent. Trade routes with the Middle and Far East, which had been open for centuries, were formalised in the late 1600s and the artifacts, textiles and garments that were imported to Europe sparked a craze for Exoticism, with cross-cultural influences becoming apparent in fashion. Indian cotton and Chinese silk became so highly prized that the huge demand for them prompted the European textile trade to advance its technological capabilities and provide the goods domestically.

The beginnings of the Industrial Revolution were apparent from early in the 18th century and although its full impact would not be felt until the 1800s, it is possible to see the nascent form of a commercialised fashion industry at this time. A number of inventions (Kay's Flying Shuttle, Arkwright's Water Frame, Hargreaves' Spinning Jenny and Cartwright's Power Loom) transformed the textile manufacturing industry; advances in the printing press meant that from the 1770s fashion magazines, which reported on and disseminated courtly style, were established in France, England and then Germany; and the consumption of fashion expanded beyond the aristocracy and the metropolitan to include the rural and the middle class thanks to improvements in communications and the increasing sophistication of small shopkeepers.

Fashion, although dominated by the aristocracy, was not exclusive to the upper classes. The clothing of the bourgeoisie and the working man reflected cultural trends and indeed, towards the end of the 18th century and symbolic of the upheaval of the French Revolution, impacted directly upon the clothing worn by the aristocracy.

For men, change in dress was most dramatic during the 17th century, particularly in England where the austere clothing favoured during the civil war was supplanted by the voluminous and highly adorned outfits that accompanied the Restoration of Charles II to the throne in 1660. However, the ensemble of breeches, waistcoat and coat (a precursor to the modern-day three-piece suit) was adopted in England, France and other areas of Europe from the 1660s and, with variations in fabric and surface decoration, dominated menswear until the French Revolution.

The 18th century was brought to a decisive close by the French Revolution in 1789, an event that acted as a catalyst for huge changes in fashion. Clothing became politicised and was used to represent the egalitarian ideology of the Revolution. The artifice and ostentation that had been a characteristic of fashions in the ancien régime were renounced in favour of simple fabrics, natural silhouettes and practicality. This change did not, however, happen overnight, and a more subtle rejection of lavish clothing had been evident since the 1770s when a trend for Naturalism became apparent and a French craze for typically restrained English sporting styles resulted in a wave of Anglomania.

↑ Peter Lely, *The Duke and Duchess of Lauderdale*, 1675. Oil on canvas; National Trust, Ham House, Richmond-upon-Thames, Twickenham, England
Portraiture of the 17th and 18th century is an excellent source of information on the fashionable clothing worn at the time. In this portrait of the Duke and Duchess of Lauderdale, the lavish clothing worn reflects their powerful status in Restoration-period England.

← Sack back gown, c 1760.
Victoria and Albert Museum, London, England
The sack back gown became the dominant style for women in the mid-18th century. It was so called because the back was loose and hung, as the name would suggest, like a sack from the shoulders. The front was open to reveal a decorative stomacher and matching petticoat. This refined and delicately ornamented silk gown displays characteristics typical of the Rococo period and the colour is one that was popular throughout the 18th century.

KEY COLLECTIONS
AUSTRIA Modesammlung des Historischen Museums, Vienna
ENGLAND Fashion Museum, Bath
FRANCE Musée de la Mode et du Textile, Louvre, Paris; Musée des Tissus et des Arts décoratifs, Lyons
ITALY Galleria del Costume, Palazzo Pitti, Florence
JAPAN Kyoto Costume Institute, Kyoto
SCOTLAND National Museum of Costume, Shambellie House, Dumfries and Galloway
SPAIN Museo del Traje, Madrid

In 1660 Charles II of England was restored to the throne, following an 11-year period of exile at the Court of Louis XIV in France. The flamboyant and lavish style that accompanied the Restoration was influenced by contemporary French fashion, but also represented the ideological triumph of the frivolous monarchy over the puritanical Commonwealth of Oliver Cromwell.

OLIVER CROMWELL (1599–1658); JOHN EVELYN (1620–1706); CHARLES II (1630–85); SAMUEL PEPYS (1633–1703); LOUIS XIV (1638–1715)

petticoat breeches; cannons; doublet; periwig; vest

The tumultuous political landscape of 17th-century Britain found expression in the clothing of the period. While under the governance of the radical puritan Oliver Cromwell, the fashion of his supporters was restrained in line, embellishment and colour. After Cromwell's death, the restoration to the throne of the exiled Charles II in 1660 prompted a fashion that was ostentatious, highly adorned and the antithesis of the relatively austere clothing it supplanted. For men in particular, fashion became increasingly flamboyant and the era was documented by a contemporary as being 'a strange effeminate age when men strive to imitate women in their apparel'. Yards of ribbon, fine lace, tassels and bows decorated the standard male aristocratic dress.

The voluminous petticoat breeches, which had been worn before the Restoration and known as Rhinegrave breeches, became universal after 1660. These were trimmed with lavish amounts of ribbon and were so wide (sometimes up to 1.8 metres/6 feet) that they were

↓ Gentleman's suit with matching cape, 1670s. Victoria and Albert Museum, London, England
This outfit comprising a coat, worn atop a vest (waistcoat) and relatively close-fitting breeches, was an early forerunner of the modern man's suit. It represents attempts to reform English dress in 1666, under the edict of Charles II, and thus distinguish it from French attire of the period.

indistinguishable from a short skirt. Around the knee, ornamental extensions called cannons were attached to the tops of stockings. These were flamboyant and deeply ruffled frills of lace or ribbon that fell like a skirt over the top of knee-length boots. The doublet, a close-fitting short jacket, was worn over a fluid cascading shirt. The effect was completed by the fashion for increasingly flamboyant, obviously artificial and highly styled wigs, or periwigs. Styles included the extremely large full-bottomed wig of neat centre parting and sausage curls which cascaded over the shoulders. This remained in fashion until the early 1700s.

In what amounted to an attempt to break away from the dominance of French fashion, from 1666 Charles II made a concerted effort to reform male dress and introduced to court a prototype of the modern-day three-piece suit. Based on a traditional Persian ensemble it comprised a long vest (what today we would recognise to be a waistcoat) and was worn under a coat of the same length (an evolution of the doublet) with relatively narrow breeches. Invaluable accounts of the adoption and dissemination of these styles were recorded by contemporary commentators Samuel Pepys and John Evelyn.

Whereas male fashion had undergone a radical transformation, for women the styles adopted during the Restoration exhibited only minor modifications from those that had been worn during the earlier Stuart monarchy. Gowns (until 1680) were still composed of a separate close-fitting, long-waisted, tightly boned bodice and skirt. However, during the Restoration period these bodices became narrower and longer at the front, and the wide and low necklines were trimmed with lace or a band of linen.

↑ Silver tissue gown, 1660–70.
Fashion Museum, Bath, England
This is a rare surviving example of costume from the Restoration period. Most probably worn for a formal occasion or to court, it is made from a highly perishable fabric called silver tissue. This is composed of fine cream silk woven with silver thread and is trimmed with parchment lace. Gowns of this period were made up of component parts. This silhouette is typical of the era and stands in contrast to the ostentation with which men dressed.

OTHER COLLECTIONS
BELGIUM Modemuseum, Hasselt
ENGLAND Museum of London, London
FRANCE Musée de la Mode et du Textile, Louvre, Paris
US The Costume Institute, Metropolitan Museum of Art, New York

 Baroque; Rococo;
New Romanticism

 Revolutionism; Neoclassicism;
Minimalism

The term Baroque was coined in the 19th century by art historians disparaging of what they considered to be a grotesque and vulgar style that lacked restraint or elegance. History has been more forgiving and it is now generally seen to be a period of lavish ornamentation, heavy curvilinear form, weighty fabrics and sombre ostentation.

The basic silhouette for women did not alter radically during the Baroque period, but the decorative detail lost its early ease and lightness to become more formal and rich. This reflected the temperament of the ageing Sun King, Louis XIV, whose reign (1661–1715) dominated the era.

Towards the end of the 17th century, for formal occasions women wore the mantua. Around 1680 this had found popularity as a simple, Middle Eastern-influenced T-shaped over-gown with an unboned bodice that could be loosely tailored to fit the body. However, its construction evolved and it became a three-piece formal gown suitable for court. The over-gown (the mantua itself) was cut in one piece from shoulder to hem and the skirts were caught up at the side to reveal a self-coloured or contrasting petticoat (what we would now call a skirt) with a longer train. A stiffened triangular stomacher provided definition. Decorative detail was plentiful and (mirroring the male fashion for extravagant wigs) a towering Fontange head-dress fashioned from upright, starched lace and ribbon found popularity.

Baroque is the name given to the style that dominated fashion, art and the decorative arts throughout the 17th century and the early part of the 18th century. Characterised by extravagant ornamentation, curvilinear design, splendour and stiffness, it was closely associated with the reign of Louis XIV of France. Upon his death, in 1715 the pageantry and formality of Baroque gave way to the more light-hearted and whimsical Rococo period.

LOUIS XIV (1638–1715); JEAN-ANTOINE WATTEAU (1684–1721); ANGÉLIQUE DE FONTANGES (1661–81)

decorative; heavy; ornate; stiff; formal; mantua; sack gown; Watteau gown

For informal wear, the flowing sack gown became popular from around 1705 to 1715. Also known as a Watteau gown, in reference to regular representation of the garment in the paintings of Jean-Antoine Watteau, this was characterised by drapes of fabric falling from pleated shoulders to the hem.

Men's clothing experienced a relatively greater transformation throughout the period. The frippery of lace, ribbon and cascading fabrics that characterised early and mid-Baroque male attire were supplanted by a much stiffer and more upholstered style that gave the impression men were extensions of the furniture they sat upon. Adding to this effect, wigs took on increasingly extravagant and somewhat cumbersome proportions. However, the major innovation of the period was the adoption, from traditional Persian costume, of coat, vest and breeches. Male attire had, for the first time, taken on a form that was recognisable as the modern-day three-piece suit.

Sir Thomas Kirkpatrick's silver embroidered coat of West of England cloth, c 1720. Fashion Museum, Bath, England

The heavy and elaborate silver embroidery, sombre colour and stiff fabric exhibited in this ensemble of around 1720 were typical of late Baroque male attire. The outfit would have been worn for formal occasions and is a style introduced by Charles II in 1666. The collarless coat, fitted to the waist and then full to the knee, worn with a waistcoat and knee-length breeches was adapted from a Persian style and was the forerunner of the modern-day three-piece suit.

↓ Woman's mantua, stomacher and petticoat, c 1700. Los Angeles County Museum of Art, Los Angeles, California, US

Just as the fabrics and fashions of the Baroque period were stiff, elaborate and heavily embellished, so the accessories and hairstyles to accompany them were equally as structured. The Fontange, or commode as it was known in England and the colonies, was a tall, peaked head-dress composed of tiers of wired and stiffened lace, around which the hair was arranged. Shown here with a formal mantua gown, it was named after Marie Angélique de Scorailles de Roussille, Duchesse de Fontanges, a favoured mistress of Louis XIV. Having lost her cap while horse riding, she hastily gathered her hair with a ribbon, thus giving birth to a style that would dominate women's formal headwear from around 1680 to 1715.

OTHER COLLECTIONS

AUSTRIA Wien Museum, Vienna
ENGLAND Victoria and Albert Museum, London
FRANCE Musée de la Mode et du Textile, Louvre, Paris
GERMANY Bavarian National Museum, Munich
ITALY Galleria del Costume, Palazzo Pitti, Florence
JAPAN Kobe Fashion Museum, Kobe
US Arizona Costume Institute, Phoenix Art Museum, Phoenix, Arizona; Museum of Art, Rhode Island School of Design, Providence, Rhode Island

Restorationism; Rococo; Exoticism

Industrialism; Modernism; Utility

Rococo – which comes from the French *rocaille,* meaning ornamental rock and shell work – broadly coincided with the reign of Louis XV (1715–74). It was a playful and decorative style that found expression in the architecture, interior design and fashions of the period, particularly in France. It was distinguished from the excessive pomp and formality of Baroque by its refinement, gaiety, lightness and prettiness.

LOUIS XV (1710–74); **MADAME DE POMPADOUR** (1721–64)

robe à la française; stomacher; *echelle;* harmony; embellishment; frivolity

Smaller and more delicate in scale than Baroque, Rococo was characterised by a florid use of naturalistic motifs, 'C' and 'S' curves, subtle colour and delicate ornament. The style, which also found expression in architecture, art and the decorative arts, translated well to fashion. Clothing during this period was elevated to an art form and was lavished with the due care and attention that indicated.

The typical Rococo gown was the *robe à la française*. This was an evolution of the sack gown, or *robe volante*, but instead of falling straight from the shoulders it had double pleats on either side of the back seam to create fullness at the rear. The front bodice was fitted and had a deep V to which was attached a stiff, triangular stomacher. This was shaped like and acted as a shield for the décolletage while providing a site for rich decorative opportunities, usually with a ladder of ribbons (*echelle*) or rich embroidery. Over-gowns were split at the front to reveal an underskirt fashioned in the same fabric and decorated with the same trimmings.

Narrow waists and wide skirts were created using corsets and panniers. Literally translated as 'basket', the pannier was a form of collapsible, boned undergarment that gave shape to the skirt. They first found favour around 1720 and dominated the female silhouette until after 1770 when the trend for Naturalism relinquished the unnatural and the unnecessary.

This silhouette did not, however, deviate radically from that which had been delineated during the Baroque period. It was in the surface detail that Rococo was distinct. Stand-away cuffs of stiff lace were replaced with hand-worked gossamer light lace ruffles or *engageantes*; the heavily gilded, sombre and weighty Baroque fabrics were supplanted by delicately harmonious, ornamented and refined textiles often influenced by the parallel trend for Exoticism; and accessories were essential and included fans, richly decorated but hidden (and thus never to be seen) pockets, head-dresses and shawls. Trimmings of ribbon, chenille, feather and artificial flowers were also essential to the Rococo style.

→ Silk brocade *robe à la française, c* 1760.
Kyoto Costume Institute, Kyoto, Japan
Technical advances made in the production of fine silks in the French town of Lyons were integral to the frivolity, lightness of touch and refinement realised during the Rococo period. Supported by the French government the silk trade became technically advanced producing textiles of such beauty that they became one of the most prized commodities in Europe. The orange silk brocade used to fashion this *robe à la française* displays a light plant pattern. Themes of nature were a common source for prints during the period.

Madame de Pompadour, the mistress of Louis XV, popularised and was an exemplar of the style. Portraits of her adorned in an elegant froth of lace and chenille perfectly capture the gaiety of the Rococo aesthetic.

Men would typically have worn the *habit à la française*. This ensemble of coat fitted at the waist, waistcoat and breeches was accessorised with silk stockings, shirt with a jabot and decorative cuffs and an elaborately knotted cravat. Exquisite textiles in rich and brilliant colours were embellished with intricate and elegant embroidery.

As for women, trimmings were important so gossamer fine lace and decorative buttons were used to finish the look.

Both sexes would have used hair powder, ribbons, fringing, buckles on high-heeled shoes and cosmetics. This was the last time in history that men and women would share decorative excess.

After 1770 the dominance of the Rococo style diminished. At court, what had been a light and elegant style gave way to vulgar extravagance based upon artifice and excess. Elsewhere, the bubbling dissatisfaction with the ancien régime found expression in a rejection of courtly styles in favour of a more appropriate, natural and liberated silhouette.

← **Cream silk mantua, 1740–45.**
Victoria and Albert Museum, London, England
Panniers, the basket-like collapsible underskirts that dictated the silhouette and volume of skirts, varied in size and shape. At court the fashion was for excessive width and an elliptical shape. As the fashion reached excess the pannier was split in two with one worn on each hip. At their most outrageous they could extend to several feet on either side. This prevented a woman from entering a room any way but sideways, made seating at the theatre and other social occasions problematic, and ensured that a woman took up three times as much space as a man.

OTHER COLLECTIONS
BELGIUM Mode Museum, Antwerp
FRANCE Musée de la Mode et du Textile, Louvre, Paris; Musée des Tissus et des Arts décoratifs, Lyons; Museum of French History, Versailles
ITALY Galleria del Costume, Palazzo Pitti, Florence
SWEDEN Nationalmuseum, Stockholm
US The Costume Institute, Metropolitan Museum of Art, New York

Baroque; Exoticism; Romanticism

Bloomerism; Brand Revivalism; Space Ageism

Exoticism is the introduction of a style or custom from another country coupled with a fascination for its alluring strangeness. Influenced by growing trade links between Europe and the Far East as well as the use of 'exotic' clothing styles in popular theatre productions, Exoticism influenced the textiles, surface decoration, silhouettes and accessories of fashionable European clothing throughout the 18th century.

MADAME DE POMPADOUR (1721–64); **CHRISTOPHE-PHILIPPE OBERKAMPF** (1738–1815)

chinoiserie; bizarre silks; Toile du Juoy; oriental

In its endless quest for novelty, European fashion has long turned to the costume, decorative arts and ephemera of non-Western, particularly Eastern, cultures for inspiration. Trade links had been established between Europe and the Far East for centuries, but were sealed in the late 17th century and a steady stream of artifacts and textiles followed. This prompted a craze for Exoticism that lasted throughout the 18th century.

The influence of Exoticism was most apparent in textiles. The Rococo love of refinement, delicate touch and harmony was embodied in exquisite Chinese painted silks depicting naturalistic blossoming flowers, leaves, birds and other flora and fauna. At a reduced price, but still bearing the incredible Chinese designs, printed cotton also found a ready market.

Inspired by the beauty of Chinese fabrics, European manufacturers set about creating their own 'Chinese' textiles. This was part of a wider craze for chinoiserie, a Western take on the imagined exoticism of the East that came not from experience but from the imagination. This was a pervasive trend that impacted on the domestic interiors of the 18th century. Bizarre silks, woven in Italy, England and France, were a strange hybrid of Chinese and Baroque elements and were popular from around 1700.

Indian textiles also known as chintz in England (from the Hindi *chint*, meaning hand-painted cotton) or *toile peinte* (hand-painted cloth) in France were also extremely popular. Aided by advances in chemistry and engineering, French manufacturing of Indiennes (for they still bore that name irrespective of provenance) took off after 1759. The most famous of these was Toile du Juoy, established by Christophe-Philippe Oberkampf in 1762.

Madame de Pompadour, the official lover of Louis XIV, did much to promote this fashion and was often painted in gowns made from Chinese painted silk and chinoiserie fabrics manufactured in Lyons, the French silk capital.

From 1772 a number of styles appeared in quick succession, all with names that alluded to an exotic pedigree. The *robes à la polonaise, à la levite, à la turque* and *à la sultane* – names so evocative of the East – tended to follow Western convention and bore only a slight relation to their exotic namesakes.

The French Revolution (1789) temporarily halted the trend for Exoticism, but it re-emerged, in another form, towards the end of the 19th century, and has had a persistent and pervasive influence on fashions of the 20th and 21st centuries.

← **Painted Chinese silk polonaise dress, *c* 1770. The Costume Institute, Metropolitan Museum of Art, New York, US**
The *robe à la polonaise* became fashionable in the 1770s. It was so called because the three draped panels that formed when the skirt was swept up with cords made reference to the first partition of Poland into three countries in 1772.

↓ **Quilted printed cotton banyan, *c* 1780. Gallery of Costume, Platt Hall, Manchester, England**
On occasion non-Western garments were incorporated into fashionable European dress. Particularly popular was the banyan. Named after a caste of Hindu merchants from the Indian subcontinent, this was a loose-fitting and comfortable dressing gown worn from the 17th century, but which later evolved into a more fitted style with set-in sleeves, similar to a man's coat. Traditionally made in Indian linen cloth they were re-imagined in flamboyant silks, calico cottons and glazed wool. The banyan became a symbol of status and wealth, and gentlemen would have their portraits painted while wearing one.

OTHER COLLECTIONS
CANADA Textile Museum of Canada, Toronto
CHINA Nantong Textile Museum, Nantong
FRANCE Musée des Tissus et des Arts décoratifs, Lyons
INDIA The Calico Museum of Textiles, Ahmedabad
JAPAN Nara National Museum, Nara
US Indiana State Museum, Indianapolis, Indiana; Philadelphia Museum of Art, Philadelphia, Pennsylvania; Textile Museum, Washington DC

Rococo; Orientalism; World Clothing

Ritualism; Savile Row; Punk

Naturalism dominated French fashion from 1780 and was marked by a rejection of artifice and pointless extravagance in favour of simplicity, comfort and functionality. It was a manifestation of the fermenting resentment felt towards the French monarchy.

 JEAN-JACQUES ROUSSEAU (1712–78); **MARIE ANTOINETTE** (1755–93); **ELISABETH LOUISE VIGÉE LE BRUN** (1755–1842)

 return to nature; simplicity; Anglomania, *robe à la anglaise*; redingote; *chemise à la reine*

 Fashion during the Rococo period (from around 1720 onwards), although refined, light-hearted and elegant, was marked by artifice. The froth of ribbons, lace and bows, the rustling and technically adroit silks, and the use of powder, wigs and cosmetics (for both sexes) combined to create a fashion that owed more to technical ingenuity than it did to Mother Nature. However, from the 1770s the frippery of Rococo was reserved for formal occasions and fashion experienced a return to nature, comfort and simplicity.

A number of political, social and cultural developments precipitated this transition to informality. The rejection of imposed

structures and conventions, as popularised by Jean-Jacques Rousseau, chimed with the fermenting antipathy felt towards the privileged aristocracy. The simplification of clothing was a symbolic rejection of the existing class structure and the inequality that imposed. In addition, unaware of their own forthcoming upheaval, French women adopted the revolutionary styles worn by women during the American Revolution (War of Independence) (1775–82). Hairstyles *à la philadelphie* and outfits of simple cotton in 'American grey' found favour with those who had abandoned the corset, panniers and powder of Rococo.

In addition, Anglomania (a French fetish for all things English) was given currency by the perception that England was a land of liberty. From 1778, for formal occasions women wore the *robe à la anglaise*, a more close-fitting, less ostentatious and cumbersome alternative to the stiff and triangular form of the *robe à la française*. The clothing worn for the traditional English pursuits of outdoor life was modified and adopted as everyday fashionable dress. The redingote was a gown adapted from an English riding jacket with collar, lapels and fitted long sleeves attached to a fitted body and full skirt. For men, Anglomania meant the adoption of functional and comfortable hats, boots and jackets based on riding outfits, and the rejection of embellishment, wigs and silk stockings.

As if to underline the vulgarity of social status as expressed through extravagant clothing, the styles worn at court became more exaggeratedly ostentatious. For example, women's hairstyles became so monumental they were able to support models of galleons in full sail, chariots and pastoral landscapes, and became home to vermin enticed by the flour paste required to stiffen them.

Philip Wickstead, *The Grand Tour Group*, 1772–3. Oil on canvas; National Trust, Springhill, The Lenox-Conyngham Collection, Magherafelt, Co Londonderry, Northern Ireland

The Grand Tour, an extended voyage around Europe taken by the English nobility for educational purposes, served to disseminate many English clothing styles to the Continent. The simple, functional and sporting lines of the male frock coat and the female riding jacket stood in contrast to the hugely embellished garments worn on the Continent at this time. As such they had a palpable effect upon local tastes and fashions.

Muslin chemise or 'creole' dress, 1780s. Gallery of Costume, Platt Hall, Manchester, England

The *chemise à la reine* or *à la creole,* so called because it resembled an undergarment of the same name, was the most distinctive women's fashion introduced in the late 18th century. It was made from simple white muslin or calico, had a raised waistline, gathered sleeves and fell straight to the floor. A portrait by Elisabeth Louise Vigée Le Brun of Marie Antoinette launched the style, but also attracted vehement criticism for the impropriety of the sheer and supposedly vulgar attire. However, this style came to dominate fashion until the return to the corset in the 1820s.

OTHER COLLECTIONS

ENGLAND Victoria and Albert Museum, London
FRANCE Museum of Costume, Avallon
ITALY Galleria del Costume, Palazzo Pitti, Florence
JAPAN Kyoto Costume Institute, Kyoto
PORTUGAL Museu Nacional do Traje e da Moda, Lisbon
US The Costume Institute, Metropolitan Museum of Art, New York; Los Angeles County Museum of Art, Los Angeles, California

Revolutionism; Neoclassicism; Dandyism

Restorationism; Baroque; Glam; Punk; Japanese Avant-Gardeism

← Man's linen shirt and cotton pantaloons and woman's jacket and petticoat, 1790s.
Kyoto Costume Institute, Kyoto, Japan
Fashion was used to identify those who supported the new social order. Silk stockings and breeches were eschewed in favour of an outfit typical of the working man, with long trousers made of rough broadcloth worn with a simple shirt and (although not shown here) a short red jacket (carmagnole), a tricolour cockade (red, white and blue rosette) worn on the side of a Phrygian cap and clogs. Those who adopted this attire were known as the *sans-culottes*, or those that did not wear breeches. Similarly, for women natural materials in simple shapes replaced lavish silks and flamboyant ornamentation.

 The French Revolution was the catalyst for a huge change in popular fashions. The lavish and unnatural lines of the Rococo period were abandoned in favour of the simplicity and Naturalism that represented the egalitarian ideology of the Revolution.

JACQUES-LOUIS DAVID (1748–1825); LOUIS XVI (1754–93); MARIE ANTOINETTE (1755–93); MAXIMILIEN ROBESPIERRE (1758–94)

simplicity; Naturalism; ideology; Reign of Terror; *sans-culottes*

The sources of the discontent that culminated in the French Revolution of 1789 were various. Extreme food shortages, economic failure and the incongruity of the extravagant court of Louis XVI and his Queen, Marie Antoinette (summed up by her apocryphal declaration 'Let them eat cake') were all contributing factors.

The inequality that had characterised the ancien régime was to be swept away and clothing was consciously politicised in order to promote and represent the ideals of the new social order. Silks were replaced with cotton, the silhouette became simplified, and ostentatious decoration was abandoned. This was not only an ideological shift; the need to distance oneself from the court was a matter of self-preservation during the Reign of Terror (September 1793 to July 1794) when enemies of the state were executed under the orders of Maximilien Robespierre.

However, this did not mark a complete break with pre-Revolution French fashion; instead it served to catalyse what had already presented itself as a general trend. For women, the Naturalism that had begun in the 1770s continued before evolving into the Neoclassical style that dominated the Directoire (1795–9) and Empire (1799–1820) periods of the Revolution. In addition, unaware of their own forthcoming upheaval, French women adopted the revolutionary styles worn by women during the American War of Independence (1775–82). Hairstyles *à la philadelphie* and outfits of simple cotton in 'American grey' found favour with those who had abandoned the corset, panniers and powder of Rococo.

For men, the egalitarian credo of the Revolution was embodied in the clothing of the *sans-culottes* (literally, without breeches). Reports vary, but it is most likely that this outfit remained almost exclusively within the domain of the working man and the street protester. Post-Revolution, an evolved version of the English riding outfit of frock coat and trousers became everyday wear for the middle classes and above. Paradoxically, the rejection of the clothing and luxurious textiles that symbolised social stratification and oppression created huge suffering within the French textile and fashion industries. And it was the working man who suffered most.

The dogmatic idealism that characterised the first part of the Revolution gave way to the Directoire period and society once again developed an interest in fashion and novelty. Fashion journals reappeared and the Neoclassical style, which chimed with the democratic tenets of Greek and Roman classical antiquity, went on to dominate fashion until 1820.

← Jacques-Louis David, *Portrait of Pierre Seriziat (1757–1847) the artist's brother-in-law*, 1795.
Oil on panel; Louvre, Paris, France
This portrait, by the exemplar of the Neoclassical style Jacques-Louis David, shows the newly typical outfit of the elegant male in 1795, the close of the first period of the Revolution. The beautifully tailored lines of the fitted trouser, the double-breasted, high-collared wool riding coat and short double-breasted waistcoat are a prototype of what would evolve to become the traditional man's suit.

OTHER COLLECTIONS
FRANCE Museum of Costume, Avallon; Museum of French History, Versailles; Musée de la Mode et du Textile, Louvre, Paris; Musée des Tissus et des Arts décoratifs, Lyons

 Neoclassicism; Bloomerism; Rationalism; Modernism; Utility; Grunge

 Restorationism; Baroque; Romanticism; New Romanticism

Neoclassicism (1795–1820), also known as the Directoire or Empire style, was a restrained, relatively simple and linear fashion that looked to the classicism of Greek and Roman antiquity for inspiration. Arguably, this radical departure from the elaborate and cumbersome outfits fashionable during the Rococo period reflected the democratic tenets of the newly founded post-Revolution French Republic.

JACQUES-LOUIS DAVID (1748–1825); **EARL SPENCER** (1758–1834); **MADAME RÉCAMIER** (1777–1849)

Directoire; Empire; classicism; Grecian; Roman; antiquity; reticules; paisley

Elements of Neoclassicism had been part of fashionable female dress from 1760. The chemise, a simple white cotton dress that derived its name from an undergarment, marked a drastic move away from the corseted, full-skirted styles of Rococo. Almost transparent, with gathered short sleeves, low décolletage and a loose tubular body, this evolved into the Neoclassical style that dominated fashion from 1795 until around 1820.

Based upon gowns seen on ancient Greek statues, fabrics were diaphanous and simple: muslin, light cotton gauze and percale gave the draped effect necessary to replicate classical styles. Such fabrics also served to further distance Neoclassical styles from the stiff, moulded textiles they supplanted. The waist moved from its natural position to settle just below the bust; corsets were abandoned;

a plain under-dress was worn to preserve modesty; and the neckline was generally square, but was certainly low. Fine, usually self-coloured embroidery provided surface decoration, and shoes, in keeping with the style of dress, were flat, light and low cut.

The lightweight and relatively simple cut of these outfits had practical implications. No longer was it possible to include pockets on a skirt so women were forced to carry small pouches or handbags. Characterised by a drawstring closure these were called reticules and were made in a multitude of

fabrics and styles, replicating anything from urns and pineapples to shells and baskets.

Also, the gauzy fabric of the Neoclassical dress was no match for the European winters and necessitated warm outer garments and accessories. Cashmere shawls became popular (and vital). Originally imported from India, machine-made lambswool replicas were made in the Scottish town of Paisley and their distinctive teardrop design became known as a paisley pattern. Paintings of fashionable women show them draping the shawls in a way that reinforces the classical connotation. A portrait of the famous and influential beauty, Madame Récamier, by Francois Gerard (1802) was particularly representative and, for some, the style became synonymous with her.

To further protect against the elements, coats and jackets, as we would recognise them today, were worn for the first time. Particularly popular was a very short tailored jacket that covered the hands and was named the Spencer (after English aristocrat Earl Spencer); this was modified for women and worn between 1795 and 1820.

By the 1820s the fashioned waist dropped to its natural position and once again women wore corsets to achieve the small-waisted ideal required of them. Not until the beginning of the 20th century would there again be a popular fashion for uncorseted (and comfortable) styles for women.

Muslin gown and shawl, 1800–11.
Victoria and Albert Museum, London, England
The popularity of the simple muslin gown and other Neoclassical styles from 1795 showed the influence of Greek and Roman antiquity upon the aesthetic of the era. An evolution of the chemise dress that had been adopted by women in the 1780s, the Neoclassical, or Empire line, gown was distinguished by its hoop-less skirt, high waistline and the use of fine muslin and cotton imported from India.

↑ Jacques-Louis David, *Portrait of Madame Raymond de Verninac (1780–1827)*, 1798–9.
Oil on canvas; Louvre, Paris, France
The paintings of Jacques-Louis David exemplify, and were instrumental in, the dissemination of the Neoclassical clothing style. His depictions of fashionable women wearing simple muslin gowns and draped with shawls (so as to underline the classical influence) had a huge impact upon the public, once again hungry for fashion and novelty in post-Revolution France.

OTHER COLLECTIONS
FRANCE Musée de la Mode et du Textile, Louvre, Paris
NORTHERN IRELAND Ulster Museum, Belfast
US Philadelphia Museum of Art, Philadelphia, Pennsylvania

Naturalism; Revolutionism; Pre-Raphaelitism;
Aestheticism; Empire Revivalism

Rococo; Romanticism; Belle Epoque;
The New Look

2

19TH CENTURY

The impact of the Industrial Revolution upon the fashions of the 19th century was all pervasive. It affected their availability, price, appearance and dissemination and generated a new social structure in which the middle classes and their values shaped cultural attitudes and thus fashion. In turn it also created pockets of resistance which rejected the ugly mechanisation, the harsh social conditions and the restrictive nature of clothing worn by women.

Industrial Revolution; rise of the middle classes; sobriety; suit; corset; crinoline; Haute Couture

Fashion in the 19th century was a reflection of both technological advancement and shifting socio-cultural attitudes towards gender and class. The Industrial Revolution, which had begun in the previous century, accelerated and although this impacted upon the production, distribution, communication and consumption of fashion its effect was felt most fully in the rise of the middle classes and the imposition of their stoic values upon the rest of society.

The development of industrial capitalism meant that wealth was no longer dependent upon heredity; hard work and a sense of purpose were, according to contemporary wisdom, the attributes that ensured a prosperous life. Hard work became a religion, thrift was encouraged and sobriety was expected. The adoption of these rigid moral codes reflected the need to find order within an era of violent social upheaval.

The values of the middle classes shaped 19th-century fashion just as the frivolity of the aristocracy had done in previous centuries. Fashion was now used to symbolise ideals of class and gender with a clear distinction between appropriate dress for men and women. This is something that has endured and shapes contemporary definitions of masculinity and femininity.

cumbersome caged crinoline; and the fabrics became fussier and more ostentatious. This restriction of women via their clothing mirrored their increasingly restricted position in society.

It was during the 19th century that the fashion industry began to take the form we recognise today with the formal establishment of the Parisian Haute-Couture industry by Charles Frederick Worth in 1868. This established the practice of producing seasonal collections and twice-yearly fashion shows as well as positioning the designer as an undisputed arbiter of style.

↖ **Carte-de-Visite taken at Chapple's studio in Ilminster, Somerset, 1864. National Trust, Killerton House, Exeter, England**
The Carte de Visite, a small professionally taken photograph measuring 2½ x 4 inches, became wildly popular after 1860. In this image the man and woman display their social status (or aspirations) through the clothes they wear; in particular the man in his restrained suit embodies the ideals of Victorian middle-class masculinity.

← **George Cruickshank, *Monstrosities of 1827* caricature, 1827. National Trust, Killerton House, Exeter, England**
The title of this caricature, showing exaggerations of fashion in the 19th century leaves the viewer in no doubt as to the attitude of its creator, George Cruickshank. Published every year from 1816 to 1828, this example satirises the fashions of 1827 and the vanity of those who wore them.

KEY COLLECTIONS
ENGLAND Fashion Museum, Bath; Victoria and Albert Museum, London
FRANCE Musée de la Mode et du Costume de la Ville de Paris, Palais Galliéra, Paris
JAPAN Kyoto Costume Institute, Kyoto
NORTHEN IRELAND Ulster Museum, Belfast
SCOTLAND National Museum of Costume, Shambellie House, Dumfries and Galloway
US Arizona Costume Institute, Phoenix Art Museum, Phoenix, Arizona; The Costume Institute, Metropolitan Museum of Art, New York

Men, it has been argued, renounced the pursuit of beauty and instead became paragons of restraint. Flamboyant male clothing with its connotations of morally reprehensible aristocratic excess (as well as effeminacy) became wholly undesirable. Instead, the fitted, dark-coloured, unembellished suit was adopted as a symbol of respectability and high-minded ideals.

At the beginning of the century the simple, linear and unrestrictive Neoclassical style dominated. However, the freedom that women experienced in these uncorseted gowns can be viewed as an aberration in the trajectory of 19th-century female fashion. As the century progressed, styles became more unwieldy and restrictive. From the 1820s the corset was reintroduced and became ever tighter; skirts got fuller and were supported first by numerous heavy petticoats and then the

◐ Dandyism was (and still is) characterised not by a particular style, but by a dedication to sartorial excellence. The original Dandy was Beau Brummell. Treated as a fashion oracle by his aristocratic contemporaries, he transformed English codes of dress and etiquette in the period 1794 to 1816. He did so by shunning ostentatious fashions in favour of fitted outfits of sober perfection.

◑ **GEORGE, PRINCE OF WALES** (1762–1830); **GEORGE BRYAN 'BEAU' BRUMMELL** (1778–1840); **ALFRED GUILLAUME GABRIEL, COUNT D'ORSAY** (1801–52); **OSCAR WILDE** (1854–1900); **TOM WOLFE** (1931–)

◑ sartorial excellence; distinction, elegance; restraint; modernity; taste

● Appearance was not an adjunct to the life of the Dandy, but was the very purpose of their being. However, clothing formed only part of the carefully constructed Dandy image. Being a Dandy depended upon fastidious but discreet personal grooming, an air of distinction, elegance and poise, a capricious attitude that allowed them to create and change their own sartorial rules, perfectly cultivated manners and, above all, a studied posture of apparent indifference. According to Baudelaire, 'the dandy is blasé or feigns to be', which in modern parlance would be referred to as 'cool' detachment.

George Bryan 'Beau' Brummell was the proto Dandy and dominated British male fashion from 1794 to 1816. Though not upper class by birth, he moved in aristocratic circles living off his wits, and used London as a stage for his restrained and paradoxically indifferent peacockery. Brummell was, however, much more than a well-dressed social climber. He was an autocratic Modernist who rejected the dominant aristocratic style of powder, wigs

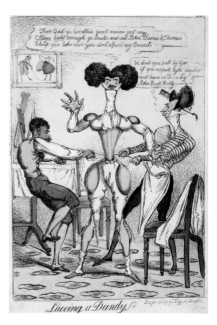

Lacing a Dandy

and high heels worn with extravagant silks, velvets and jewels, instead promoting a look that was extreme in its apparent restraint. His sphere of influence was enhanced when he became close to the Prince of Wales (the future King George IV) and the arbiter of courtly fashions as well as etiquette.

Brummell's favoured attire was a development of the practical, tailored clothing worn for hunting and other equestrian and leisure pursuits. He wore an expertly cut dark coat, usually in blue, with swallowtails; his adoption of tight-fitting breeches was instrumental in popularising trousers for men; the leather riding boots that were worn for daytime were polished to perfection; and his concession to mild ostentation was an elaborately tied linen neck cloth worn under a high and stiff shirt neck. His 'Titus' haircut of short curls with long sideburns and clean-shaven, well-scrubbed skin inferred a lack of concern when in fact hours were spent perfecting such insouciance.

Advances in textile manufacturing and tailoring techniques enabled Brummell's sartorial exactitude. Newly developed woven woollen cloths were pliable enough to achieve the close fit and exacting cut he demanded, and London's Savile Row was at the forefront of appropriate tailoring developments.

As a philosophy, Dandyism persisted and each era and region has given rise to its own set of Dandies. The French-born Count D'Orsay supplanted Brummell as the authority on matters of taste after his move to London in 1821; during the 1890s the aesthete Oscar Wilde affected the necessary reverence for appearance while maintaining a lofty disdain; and the stylishly detached demeanour of writer Tom Wolfe marks him out as one of the great Dandies of the 20th century.

Lacing a Dandy, 1819–46.
Illustration; Museum of London, London, England
The Dandy and his narcissistic proclivities were a source of great mirth for satirists. This depiction of a Dandy having his stays pulled by a barber and a black servant derides the subject in a number of ways. The use of the male corset to temper his round figure and thus conform to a fashionably slim silhouette mocks the excessively laborious process involved in the affectation of what was an apparently refined and restrained image. And the presence of the black servant, as well as denoting links to the lucrative colonial economy, was a common device used to highlight the absurdity of what was commonly held to be sophisticated behaviour.

↓ Men's standard dress, 1820s.
Victoria and Albert Museum, London, England
The combination of tight breeches, fitted waistcoat and expertly cut coat which had been a subversive sartorial statement in the late 1790s when first promoted by Beau Brummell had, with some modifications, been adopted as the male standard form of dress by the early 1820s. By this time the collar, lapels and extravagantly tied neckwear had been toned down and it became fashionable to wear, or appear to wear, more than one waistcoat at a time. In this example a slip waistcoat edged in red satin is worn underneath another of beige, hand-stitched poplin.

OTHER COLLECTIONS
AUSTRIA Modesammlung des Historischen Museums, Vienna
ENGLAND Fashion Museum, Bath,
FRANCE Museum of Costume, Avallon
US The Costume Institute, Metropolitan Museum of Art, New York

Neoclassicism; Savile Row; Aestheticism; Modernism; New Edwardianism; Football Casualism

Rococo; Orientalism; Existentialism

A reaction to the excessive rationality of the Enlightenment and emphasising emotion, ethereality and sensitivity, Romanticism dominated fashion, as well as other arts, in the period from around 1820 to 1850. An exaggerated silhouette, it was characterised by full 'leg o' mutton' sleeves, yawning necklines, puffed-out skirts and unnaturally small waists. Women once again stepped back into their corsets having only just relinquished them during the Neoclassical period.

SIR WALTER SCOTT (1771–1832); **LORD GEORGE GORDON BYRON** (1788–1824); **MARY SHELLEY** (1797–1851)

anti-Rationalism; dreamlike; ethereal; emotion; corset; gigot; 'leg o' mutton' sleeves; frock coat

By around 1820, almost all evidence of the rational and egalitarian aesthetic prompted by the French Revolution had been supplanted by the poetic and unashamedly pretty Romantic style. Women aspired to attain a dreamlike, ethereal quality in demeanour as well as dress. This preoccupation reflected the popularity of Anglo and Scottish romantic

→ **Day dress, 1830–35.**
Victoria and Albert Museum, London, England
Distinctive to Romantic female fashions were the gigantic gigot, or 'leg o' mutton' sleeves. Full at the top they were gathered into the shoulder and tapered towards the wrist. These peaked in volume in 1835. Hoops were sometimes used to create the necessary volume to give the appearance that the sleeves had been puffed up by bellows. More often, though, down-filled pads were attached to the upper arm to create a contour over which the sleeve could billow. Variations of the trend existed, and each pattern was assigned a name that reflected the Romantic aspirations of the era: for example, 'Donna Maria', 'Medici' and 'Sultan'.

literature, particularly in France. The work of Sir Walter Scott, Lord Byron and Mary Shelley fuelled a Continental longing for romantic escapism and provided women and men with emotionally wrought characters to emulate.

It could reasonably be argued that the preoccupation with the poetic and dreamlike was a means of escape from the immediate and pragmatic realities of industrialisation as well as a reaction against the excessive Rationalism of the Enlightenment.

As with the literature, theatre, furniture and art of the era, Romantic clothing took reference from the past. Characteristics from the Renaissance, Gothic, Rococo and particularly the Restoration periods contributed to the style. Waistlines, which had been raised during the Neoclassical period, once again settled back to their natural position and, after a short reprieve, women stepped back into the corset. The slight shortening of skirts, which now puffed out gently to form a bell shape, revealed the ankle and prompted a trend for stockings embellished with elaborate designs and jewel-coloured silk slippers with narrow, squared-off toes adorned with a small bow or a rosette. Dresses were decorated with trimmings and embroidered with romantic motifs such as rosebuds. Atop the head sat equally romantic bonnets decorated with ribbons, or wide and elaborate hairstyles were festooned with feathers, flowers and other such trimmings.

It was considered unbecoming for a woman to exhibit bawdy good health, and a melancholic air and wan pallor was cultivated in keeping with the ethereal objectives of Romantic fashion. Delicacy was favoured over strength, and fainting as a symbol of emotional turmoil was considered most fitting. For men the affectation of a brooding and poetic demeanour was cultivated.

As the 1840s approached, the excesses of the Romantic period began to wane. Sleeves assumed more normal proportions, colours became more conservative, wide hats were modified to become contour-following bonnets, and the elaborate hairstyles gave way to face-framing ringlets. However, the waistlines continued to reduce and the skirts got wider; the proportions were such that the crinoline had to be introduced to support the excessive skirt size. What had begun as a romantic style dedicated to escapism was evolving into the extremely restrictive, health-threatening silhouette of the Victorian era.

← Frock coat, 1828–30.
Victoria and Albert Museum, London, England
For men, the Romantic mood was expressed through cut and fabric. Frock coats mirrored the exaggerated female silhouette by emphasising full shoulders (though nowhere near the proportions of the gigot sleeve), narrow waists and a full skirt that exhibited volume to the rear. Velvet trimmings added to the Romantic aesthetic.

OTHER COLLECTIONS
AUSTRIA Modesammlung des Historischen Museums, Vienna
BELGIUM Mode Museum, Antwerp
ENGLAND Abington Park Museum, Nottingham; Gallery of Costume, Platt Hall, Manchester; Fashion Museum, Bath
US Arizona Costume Institute, Phoenix Art Museum, Phoenix, Arizona; The Costume Institute, Metropolitan Museum of Art, New York; National Museum of American History, Smithsonian Institution, Washington DC

 Restorationism; Rococo; Exoticism; Pre-Raphaelitism; Nostalgic Romanticism

 Revolutionism; Bloomerism; Modernism; Deconstructionism; Grunge

BCT

Until the turn of the 19th century, fashion had operated steadily, with political, social and religious upheavals operating as fashion bellwethers. The industrialisation of textile production, followed by developments in the retail and manufacturing of clothing, introduced new catalysts for the evolution of fashion: availability, affordability, social mobility and novelty on the part of the consumer, and profit on the part of the supplier.

WALTER HUNT (1796–1859); ISAAC MERRITT SINGER (1811–75); ELIAS HOWE (1819–67); SIR WILLIAM HENRY PERKIN (1838–1907)

mechanisation; dissemination; urbanisation; consumer revolution; aniline dyes

The invention of mechanised spinning, weaving and cylinder printing increased the volume, multiplied the range and reduced the cost of available textiles. As a consequence, the wardrobes of the wealthy, the newly expanded middle classes and occasionally the working classes (for Sunday best) became more varied and fashions more fast paced.

The availability of fashion for the masses was further increased by the refinement of the sewing machine (which had first been developed by Walter Hunt and then by Elias Howe) by Isaac Merritt Singer in 1851. It was immediately made available for purchase by instalments and thus became a viable proposition for the average household. Although it would be a long time before true mass production of clothing could take place, there was, from the 1860s, a rise in the number of workshops dedicated to ready-made clothing and dressmaking services.

Parallel improvements in the speed and quality of the printing press, and lower production costs, impacted directly upon the dissemination and availability of fashion. Paper patterns enhanced the quality of home-made garments and brought popular styles to the majority of the population. Journals dedicated to fashion were widely circulated, making it a more accessible and popular pastime.

The consumer revolution that accompanied and stimulated the Industrial Revolution was embodied by the rise of the department store. Here the fruits of mechanisation were peddled to the newly affluent consumer classes, agog at the wealth of styles available to them. However, while some benefited, others found they were living lives of abject misery in the rapidly expanding and ill-prepared urban centres. Appalling injustice occurred at all stages of fashion production: the UK sold African slaves to the US to finance and facilitate its lucrative cotton industry; small children, whose size and agility made them particularly useful, would work long hours for pennies and suffer horrific injuries in the unsafe machinery; and it was common for unscrupulous factory owners to not pay staff for supposedly shoddy work and then sell the goods anyway. Outside of the factories, sweatshops increased in number.

Pockets of resistance and, sometimes, denial, resulted. The ethereal, delicate and unashamedly pretty fashions of the earlier Romantic era (1820–40) symbolised a wish to escape from the harsh realities of industrialisation. In addition, the Arts and Crafts Movement, sensitive to the (relatively) crude techniques of factory production and the renunciation of refined and age-old crafts engendered by mechanisation, operated a manifesto that stressed the importance of aestheticism, individuality and the handmade.

Back detail of taffeta bodice and skirt, c 1869.
Victoria and Albert Museum, London, England
Visually, the effects of industrialisation on fashion found their greatest expression in the development of man-made aniline dyes. While trying to find a useful by-product from the distillation of coal in 1856, William Henry Perkin inadvertently created a brilliant-purple dye. Known as 'Perkin's mauve' it was a craze in fashion for a number of years. Brilliant blues, magenta and red followed and were quickly adopted by the newly empowered middle classes.

Blue silk day dress, mid- to late 1860s.
McCord Museum of Canadian History, Montreal, Canada
The wide availability of the sewing machine from 1851 impacted directly upon the appearance as well as the means of producing clothing, and dresses were increasingly festooned with extravagant ornamentation. This example is part machine- and part handmade. The mechanisation of garment production did not do away with hand work altogether, and the two coexisted for quite some time.

OTHER COLLECTIONS
ENGLAND Bradford Industrial Museum, Bradford; Fashion Museum, Bath; Gallery of Costume, Platt Hall, Manchester
NORTHERN IRELAND Ulster Museum, Belfast
US Arizona Costume Institute, Phoenix Art Museum, Phoenix, Arizona; Chicago History Museum, Chicago, Illinois; The Museum at the Fashion Institute of Technology, New York

Mass Productionism; Modernism; Globalism

Romanticism; Aestheticism; Surrealism

Just as Paris established an infrastructure and renown for its dressmaking during the 19th century and came to dominate womenswear, so London became the exemplar of world-class tailoring and, thus, menswear. Savile Row, the centre of the London tailoring community since the late 18th century, has become a byword for superlative craftsmanship, impeccable fit and the very essence of masculine sartorial propriety.

GEORGE BRYAN 'BEAU' BRUMMELL (1778–1840); HENRY POOLE (1814–76); TOMMY NUTTER (1943–92); OZWALD BOATENG (1968–)

tailoring; fit; restraint; elegance; quality

The evolution of Savile Row and the impeccable reputation of its tailors was granted by political circumstance, powerful patronage and technological advances. The French Revolution of 1789 prompted a rejection of ostentatious dress for men as clothing was politicised to represent the ideals of the new social order. Anglomania (a French fetish for all things English) was given currency by the perception that England was a land of liberty and the clothing worn for the traditional English pursuit of hunting was modified and adopted as everyday fashionable dress.

George Bryan 'Beau' Brummell, Dandy and arbiter of London style at the turn of the 18th century, also favoured a silhouette based upon practical, tailored clothing worn for hunting. His influence over the Prince of Wales and the rest of the English Court encouraged them to reject the use of powder, wigs and high heels in favour of fitted outfits of sober perfection. Ironically it was the mechanisation of the textile industry that allowed Savile Row and British hand-tailoring to flourish. Newly developed woven woollen cloths were pliable enough to achieve an exacting fit and Savile Row was at the forefront of appropriate tailoring developments.

Although the surrounding area had been home to tailoring and its attendant industries for some time, it was when Henry Poole and Co moved their entrance to Savile Row (from Old Burlington Street) in 1846 that the foundations were laid for its worldwide reputation. Also renowned for inventing the tuxedo, Henry Poole has become known as 'the founding father of Savile Row'.

Savile Row has retained its (well deserved) reputation as the home of fine tailoring. However, the continual decline of its customer base, the rising rents and a lessening pool of appropriately skilled tailors has posited a threat to its future. Diversification into ready-to-wear as well as semi-bespoke offerings has helped to revitalise the area.

Tommy Nutter, Blue check suit, 1969.
Victoria and Albert Museum, London, England
Defined by restraint, elegance and quality, Savile Row can reasonably be considered immune to the caprices of fashion. However, there have been intermittent efforts to modernise its aesthetic and culture. Tommy Nutter opened his establishment, Nutter's, on Valentine's Day 1969 and successfully broke with tradition when he combined contemporary style with traditional and accomplished techniques. His client base included Mick and Bianca Jagger, the Beatles and Yoko Ono, as well as members of the aristocratic establishment. As such it challenged the contemporary perception of what Savile Row stood for. This tradition has since been continued by Richard James, Ozwald Boateng and Timothy Everest.

▸ Ozwald Boateng, Suit, 1996.
Victoria and Albert Museum, London, England
Ozwald Boateng opened his own shop in 1995 and has gone on to embody the 21st-century character of Savile Row: commercial innovation combined with traditional techniques. This wool and mohair suit is typical of his work in which vibrant colour and up-to-the-minute styling are key components.

OTHER COLLECTIONS
AUSTRALIA Powerhouse Museum, Sydney
ENGLAND State Apartments and Royal Ceremonial Dress Collection, Kensington Palace, London
ITALY Galleria del Costume, Palazzo Pitti, Florence
US The Costume Institute, Metropolitan Museum of Art, New York

Naturalism; Neoclassicism; Dandyism; New Edwardianism

Restorationism; Rococo; Glam

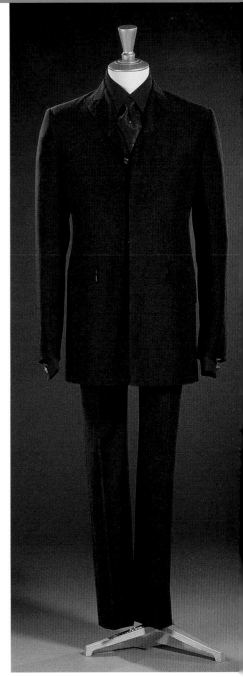

Charles Frederick Worth is credited with founding and formalising the modern Haute-Couture industry, crystallising the role of the designer as an arbiter of style and raising the status of dressmaking from anonymous trade to artistic endeavour. His superior skills, business acumen and cultivated air of exclusivity afforded him a status hitherto unseen in the fashion industry.

ROSE BERTIN (1747–1813); **CHARLES FREDERICK WORTH** (1826–95); **EMPRESS EUGÉNIE** (1826–1920); **GASTON WORTH** (1853–1924)

marchandes de modes; royal patronage; crinoline; La Chambre Syndicale de la Couture Parisienne

Although by 1858 Paris had a well-developed fashion industry, its structure was markedly different to current models. The role of the Paris dressmaker was a lowly one, accorded by Trade Guild policies established as far back as 1675, and they exerted little or no influence over prevailing fashions. It was the *marchandes de modes* (suppliers of trimmings) who were the source of sartorial authority. Rose Bertin was the most celebrated of these and her influence on fashion in pre-Revolution France was without parallel, her position being assured when she became chief fashion advisor to Marie Antoinette. Although Bertin did not design clothes per se, her success provided a context into which Haute Couture and the fashion system we recognise today were able to flower.

It is to the Englishman Charles Frederick Worth that credit is given for delineating the structure of the Paris fashion industry. Having worked for the finest textile merchants in England and France, Worth had already developed a profound understanding of fashion commerce by the time he came to open his own business on Rue de la Paix, Paris, in 1858. From the outset he cultivated an exclusive image. In contrast to existing dressmakers he elevated his own status to that of an artist to whose judgement his customers were forced to defer. Coupled with his unparalleled dressmaking skills, this earned his creations the nomenclature 'Haute Couture' – literally, high dressmaking.

After initial resistance Worth's reputation and success were cemented when Empress Eugénie, wife of Napoléan III, admired one of his creations and instructed him to supply her with gowns. So impressed was she that by 1864 Worth had become responsible for all her state- and evening wear. Considering that state balls were frequent, no gown could be worn twice and with most ladies wishing to emulate the Empress, Worth could easily be asked to supply in excess of a thousand different gowns for a single event. Not only did this demonstrate his extraordinary popularity and efficiency, but

→ Franz Xavier Winterhalter, *Elizabeth, Empress of Austria,* 1865. Oil on canvas; Kunsthistorisches Museum, Vienna, Austria
Charles Frederick Worth did more than any other to secure the reputation of Paris as the capital of world fashion and his gowns were in demand internationally. This lavish gown is typical of Worth's silhouette and displays the use of the crinoline cage, an innovation that he boldly and misleadingly took credit for inventing.

← Charles Frederick Worth, Evening dress, *c* 1887; Jean-Phillipe Worth, Evening dress, *c* 1892. The Costume Institute, Metropolitan Museum of Art, New York, US

The flat-fronted and full-backed crinoline was definitely a Charles Frederick Worth innovation. Not only did this prove to be more practical than the excessive circumference of the traditional crinoline, it also provided a new focus for fashionable decoration upon the rear of the gown. This style became widely copied, but the use of lavish fabrics, detailed ornamental embroidery and sweeping drapery distinguished Worth's designs.

also his incredible powers of innovation. Worth's designs were characterised by his use of lavish materials, and his early gowns were distinguished by the use of the crinoline. Historical references are also evident in his designs and were likely influenced by time spent perusing the art galleries of London and Paris. 'Leg o' mutton' sleeves, his last great contribution to the fashion of the 19th century, were based on those worn in the Elizabethan era.

Worth's legacy to the contemporary Haute-Couture industry has been great. In 1868 he founded an association of couture houses dedicated to regulating and protecting the work of Parisian couturiers. This was solidified by his son Gaston, and evolved into La Chambre Syndicale de la Couture Parisienne, which continues to govern the contemporary Haute-Couture industry. The Parisian Haute-Couture industry is today situated in the environs of Rue de la Paix, the address of Worth's original business.

OTHER COLLECTIONS
AUSTRIA Modesammlung des Historischen Museums, Vienna
ENGLAND Museum of London, London
RUSSIA State Hermitage Museum, St Petersburg
SCOTLAND National Museum of Scotland, Edinburgh
SPAIN Museo del Traje, Madrid
US Brooklyn Museum, New York; Cornell Costume and Textile Collection, Cornell University, Ithaca, New York; Museum of the City of New York, New York; Museum of Fine Arts, Boston, Massachusetts; State Historical Society of Wisconsin, Madison, Wisconsin

 Rococo; Belle Epoque; The New Look; The Death of Couture

 Rationalism; Mass Productionism; Modernism; Minimalism

The adoption of particular dress during the social rituals of marriage and mourning has been a constant in fashion history. However, throughout the reign of Queen Victoria (1837–1901) the codes pertaining to mourning dress and ritual became hugely complicated. During the same period, white wedding dresses, although not governed by the same strict etiquette, became extremely fashionable.

PRINCE ALBERT (1819–61); **QUEEN VICTORIA** (1819–1901)

prescriptive; complex; social etiquette; full mourning; half mourning; crape; bombazine; white wedding; virtue

Victorian society was bound by social ritual and highly complex codes of etiquette, adherence to which would denote one's sense of propriety, a characteristic highly prized by the Victorians. This was influenced by Queen Victoria who, following the death of her husband Prince Albert in 1861, remained in mourning for the rest of her life.

Mourning was divided into distinct periods, known as full, second, ordinary and, finally, half mourning with each lasting a proscribed amount of time. The length varied according to one's relationship to the deceased, but women, as was typical of the patriarchal Victorian era, faced much more rigid and all-encompassing constraints than men: a widow had to spend a total of two and a half years publicly mourning her husband; yet a man for his wife had to (ostensibly) mourn for only three months, and mourning dress often amounted to no more than a crape armband.

Women, on the other hand, were faced with a mind-boggling list of rules dictating what they could wear, how they should wear it and in which circumstance. The strict specifications pertained to elements such as fabric, cut, silhouette, buttons, underwear, trimmings and accessories. Crape (a matt silk gauze) or bombazine (a matt silk worsted weave) were the permitted fabrics for full mourning, while the addition of dull silk was allowed for second mourning. By the time half mourning was reached, shades including grey, mauve, violet, pansy and, of course, black became permissible.

The white wedding dress has been a conventional choice since the medieval period, but was by no means the only option. However, by the mid-19th century white had become the only acceptable colour for a woman who wished to demonstrate her social standing and virtue. As with her influence on mourning dress, the wedding of Queen Victoria was key to popularising the use of white.

These ideals were not universally upheld, and the prohibitive expense of full mourning or wedding dress precluded its use by a sizable proportion of society. For weddings, a smart day dress was the usual option, and coloured fabrics were used either alone or mixed with the more fashionable – and expensive – white. For mourning the issue was more problematic. The inability to mourn 'properly' was a source of extreme shame and, although not always possible, every effort was made to ensure that a semblance of the ritual was adhered to.

The fashion for the white wedding dress has persisted with full-skirted Victorian styles retaining popularity to the present day. The cult of extreme mourning was not, however, to extend beyond the First World War when the unparalleled loss of life meant that a more realistic mourning ritual was adopted.

Richard Redgrave, *Throwing Off Her Weeds*, 1846. Oil on panel; Victoria and Albert Museum, London, England

Although a woman could discard her black mourning clothes (also known as widow's weeds) after a period of two years if mourning for a husband, it was not uncommon for them to be worn long after propriety dictated. Not so the woman depicted in this painting. She is keen to discard the weeds for a lilac dress appropriate to half mourning. Her haste is indicated by the visual clues that she is again to marry: the orange blossom (a flower traditionally carried at weddings) and the bridal bonnet in the hatbox.

Wedding dress, 1864. The Costume Institute, Metropolitan Museum of Art, New York, US

Wedding dresses tended to follow the dominant fashion of their time. In this case the use of a crinoline (hooped skirt) with more volume to the back was typical of contemporary fashions that had evolved from the bell-shaped crinoline of the 1850s.

OTHER COLLECTIONS

AUSTRALIA National Gallery of Victoria, Melbourne
BELGIUM Modemuseum, Hasselt
ENGLAND Brighton Museum and Art Gallery, Brighton; Fashion Museum, Bath; Gallery of Costume, Platt Hall, Manchester; Geffrye Museum, London; National Trust, Killerton House, Exeter; Whitby Literary and Philosophical Society, Whitby; Worthing Museum and Art Gallery, Worthing; York Castle Museum, York
JAPAN Kyoto Costume Institute, Kyoto
SPAIN Museo del Traje, Madrid
US National Museum of American History, Smithsonian Institution, Washington DC

 Industrialism; Belle Epoque; Victorian Revivalism

 Glam; Punk; The Internet

Devised to aid the comfort of women, the Bloomer costume was adopted by reformers of women's dress in 1851. Named after the American feminist Amelia Jenks Bloomer, the outfit consisted of a full knee-length dress worn atop billowing, oriental-style pants gathered at the ankle. However, the outfit was quickly abandoned by feminists who felt that the severe ridicule it engendered undermined the social reform it sought to promote.

ELIZABETH CADY STANTON (1815–1902);
AMELIA JENKS BLOOMER (1818–94);
SUSAN B ANTHONY (1820–1906);
ELIZABETH SMITH MILLER (1822–1911)

dress reform; feminism; *The Lily*; *Punch* magazine; bifurcated

As the dress of Victorian women became more elaborate and cumbersome, murmurs of protest were voiced by various groups. These dress reformers sought to liberate women from the excesses of the Victorian silhouette, remove class difference and redress gender inequality. The origins of this dissent can be traced to the French Revolution, and in the early part of the 19th century became associated with religious and progressive communities in the US and France.

But it was the Bloomer costume that became one of the most famous attempts at dress reform during the 19th century. Originally known as the Turkish trouser costume, Bloomer costume consisted of billowing pantaloon-style trousers gathered with a lace frill or tie at the hem, a full-skirted tunic that fell to just below the knee, and a simplified non-restrictive bodice with a sash to shape the waist: all accessorised with soft leather boots and a wide, low-brimmed hat.

Although not originated by her (this honour goes to Elizabeth Smith Miller), the fashion was named after American feminist Amelia Jenks Bloomer. In 1848, inspired by fellow suffragettes and temperance campaigners Elizabeth Cady Stanton and Susan B Anthony, Bloomer launched *The Lily*, her own newspaper devoted to women's issues including fashion. Due to the evangelical zeal with which she promoted and defended the outfit within the publication, her name has ever since been synonymous with the Bloomer costume.

Although a more comfortable alternative to the heavy and restrictive petticoated dresses worn by contemporary women, this relatively modest attempt at dress reform provoked an inordinate surge of vitriol and ridicule. *Punch* magazine, the British satirical weekly publication, was particularly disparaging. Cartoons, conveying both amusement and consternation, portrayed the supposed absurdity of 'Bloomers' and emphasised the perceived threat to a highly patriarchal Victorian society. The captions attached to these satirical depictions of men emasculated by women in bifurcated garments left the reader in no doubt that Bloomerism was an absurd proposition. A typical caption read: 'One of the delightful results of Bloomerism – the ladies will pop the question.'

The mass derision hastened the demise of what had been a very short-lived but notorious fashion. The Bloomer costume was abandoned as counter-productive to the very cause it sought to promote. Appropriately, Amelia Bloomer was one of the last to sport the outfit, but had abandoned it by 1859. However, having been mocked throughout her life for the pantaloon style that bore her name, Bloomer was vindicated in the late 1890s when bifurcated garments for women became acceptable attire while cycling.

Music sheet featuring illustration of Amelia
Bloomer, 'I want to be a Bloomer' sung by
Miss Rebecca Isaacs, words by Henry Abrahams,
music by WH Montgomery, 1860s

Considering that the Bloomer costume was worn
by only a tiny proportion of women for a very short
period of time, the pantaloon and tunic ensemble had
a disproportionate hold on the public imagination.
Cartoons and articles ridiculing the outfit were a source
of great mirth while wry (but not wholly unflattering)
music-hall songs, such as 'I want to be a Bloomer'
further fuelled the ceaseless mocking that Amelia
Bloomer and her acolytes endured.

OTHER COLLECTIONS
Although there are numerous illustrations of
the Bloomer costume in existence, no actual
garments have survived.
US Seneca Falls Historical Society Archive Collection,
Seneca Falls, New York (contains ephemera but
no clothes)

 Pre-Raphaelitism; Rationalism;
Arts and Crafts; Existentialism

 Rococo; The Birth of Haute Couture;
Belle Epoque; The New Look

◔ A simplified version of women's dress worn over a natural, uncorseted figure, this style was mainly adopted by the wives and models of the Pre-Raphaelite Brotherhood and their circle from the 1850s to the 1870s. Their ideas continued to have a far-reaching influence on mainstream fashion into the early 20th century.

◑ **GF WATTS** (1817–1904); **DANTE GABRIEL ROSSETTI** (1828–82); **JANE MORRIS** (1839–1914); **ARTHUR LASENBY LIBERTY** (1843–1917); **MARY ELIZA HAWEIS** (1848–98)

◕ uncorseted; medieval; Watteau pleat; loose-fitting; 'art' colours

● From the 1830s onwards, European movements in dress reform reflected developments in art, literature, philosophy and politics. Members of the Pre-Raphaelite Brotherhood, a group of artists whose admiration of medieval painting and craftsmanship reflected dissatisfaction with the modern manufactures celebrated by the International Exhibition of 1851, advocated 'truth to nature and beauty in all things'. They entered the philosophical debate about dress in 1848, promoting a corset-free, fluid and thus less restrictive and more healthy mode of dress for women through their paintings.

The representations of women in the works of the Pre-Raphaelite artists Dante Gabriel Rossetti, JE Millais and Edward Burne Jones were to prove inspirational to both contemporary and later groups of dress reformers, and promoted what became known as 'Artistic dress'. Models in their paintings were dressed in costumes derived from Camille Bonnard's *Costume Historique*, published in Paris in 1829–30. Other garments with less obvious historical features were made up for everyday wear, but all shared a loose-fitting and apparently simple silhouette in muted natural or 'art' colours that did not require close-fitting undergarments and rejected the dominant fashion of the time: a tight corset, rustling fabrics, cumbersome crinolines and deep artificial colours.

The lack of corsetry meant that wearers of Artistic dress were characterised as loose and thus immoral by their contemporaries, as a lack of lacing equated to a lack of modesty in the Victorian era.

Commerce also played a part. From 1875, fluid, subtle, vegetable-dyed silk and woollen textiles imported by Arthur Lasenby

← John R Parsons, *Jane Morris, posed by Rossetti*, 1865. Photograph; Victoria and Albert Museum, London, England
Jane, the wife of the influential designer and socialist William Morris, was sketched and painted by Rossetti on many occasions in the 1860s and 1870s, wearing a loose-fitting one-piece silk robe. The neckline and sleeve ends are discreetly trimmed with braid or embroidery and the full sleeves are faintly reminiscent of Renaissance dress.

Liberty from Asia for sale at his East India House establishment were admired by artists including Rossetti. Outside the Pre-Raphaelites' immediate circle, Artistic dress also coincided with an appreciation of classical form and draperies, and a craze for goods imported from Japan. Japanese dress was not promoted as an alternative to fashionable clothing but, along with classical dress, was loose fitting and appealed to artists. These clothes are depicted on artists' models of the later 1870s, in paintings by James Abbott McNeill Whistler and Lord Frederic Leighton.

The effect of the clothing worn in artistic circles on mainstream fashion was enduring and is reflected in the writing of Mrs Mary Eliza Haweis for *The Queen* magazine, a widely distributed and influential fashion publication, and in her book *The Art of Dress*, published in 1879, which features her interpretation of the 'Pre-Raphaelite' revival of medieval dress 20 years after the movement began.

The masculine version of Artistic dress, a velvet jacket and floppy bow at the neck as worn by Rossetti himself, had its roots in the Romantic movement of the early 19th century.

OTHER COLLECTIONS
ENGLAND The National Portrait Gallery, London; Tate Britain, London; Watts Gallery, Compton, Guildford

Aestheticism; Rationalism; Arts and Crafts

Space Ageism; New Romanticism; Celebrity Consumerism

↑ GF Watts, *Jane Elizabeth (Jeanie) Hughes, Mrs Nassau Senior,* 1857–8. National Trust, Wightwick Manor, Wolverhampton, England
The colour of the sitter's free-flowing locks contrasts with the vivid violet-blue dress with natural waistline and full, loose, lace-edged sleeves. Mrs Nassau Senior, a friend of Watts and Rossetti, was a campaigner for women's rights.

fluid; smocking; Liberty;
muted colours; *Punch* magazine;
bohemian; beauty; natural motifs

Taking their cue from the artistic dress
and style portrayed in Pre-Raphaelite
paintings, female advocates of Aesthetic
dress wore their hair long, somewhat frizzy
and pushed forward over the eyes; the long,
fluid and usually uncorseted dresses
eschewed frippery in favour of smocking or
simple embroidery and had loose or wide
sleeves that referenced medieval clothing;
and soft cottons, velvets and Liberty silks in
colours derived from natural vegetable dyes
were rich and muted half-tones of yellow,
peacock blue, cinnamon, sage green and
gold. A typical female aesthete was
described by a contemporary as 'a wan,
super-browed woman, with a throat like
Juno', while another noted that 'all women
look wan, untidy, picturesque, like figures of
Pre-Raphaelite women with unkempt hair'.

Women were lampooned for their
dishevelled and consumptive appearance
while men were portrayed as over-refined,
lacking in vigour and devoid of the qualities
admired in a stoic Victorian gentleman.
Cartoons by George du Maurier in *Punch*
magazine, the British satirical weekly
publication, were particularly disparaging.
The effete, stooped figure of the aesthete
man was drawn in such a way as to
question his masculinity while the women
were portrayed as slightly unhinged and
unattractive specimens. As a man who was
acquainted with a number of Aesthetes, du
Maurier drew upon first-hand observations
in his cartoons. The Aesthetes were also a
source of merriment for Gilbert and
Sullivan, whose operetta *Patience* set out to
ridicule the Aesthetic movement. Indeed,
the main character was based on leading
aesthete Oscar Wilde.

During the 1880s, a number of dress
reform movements called for female
emancipation from the bondage of corset,
bustle and high heels. Just like their
contemporaries in the Rational Dress
Society (established in London in 1881)
advocates of Aesthetic dress were opposed
to the highly restrictive and cumbersome
fashions of the day. However, they
distinguished themselves by advocating
beauty as being of equal importance to
Rationalism.

ARTHUR LASENBY LIBERTY (1843–1917);
GEORGE DU MAURIER (1834–96);
MRS JOSEPH COMYNS CARR (1850–1927);
MARY AUGUSTA WARD (1851–1920); OSCAR
WILDE (1854–1900); CONSTANCE WILDE
(1858–98)

Aesthetic dress was only ever worn by a small, bohemian and usually privileged sector of society. Key figures included Mary Augusta Ward (a popular novelist) and Mrs Joseph Comyns Carr (whose husband was director of the fashionable Grosvenor Gallery). However, it did have some influence upon mainstream fashion, particularly among the middle and upper classes. Tea gowns became popular and were, in essence, a more fashionable version of classic Aesthetic dress, and by 1910 Paris, still the world centre of fashion, was (consciously or otherwise) taking its cue from these middle-class bohemians.

Napoleon Sarony,
*Portrait photo
of Oscar Wilde*, 1882.
Albumen panel print;
National Portrait Gallery,
London, England
As well as being an exemplar of male Aestheticism, Oscar Wilde also lectured widely, promoting Aesthetic costume as a rational and attractive alternative to prevalent fashions. He suggested that clothing should hang from the shoulders rather than the waist; that if high heels were worn then the ball of the foot should be elevated to relieve pressure; that the body should remain as free as possible, thus engendering better health and greater beauty; and that contemporary clothing would do well to take inspiration from the classical lines of antiquity. His wife Constance was also an active dress reformer.

↓ Liberty robe, 1897.
Victoria and Albert Museum, London, England
In 1884 Liberty and Co of Regent Street (owned by Arthur Lasenby Liberty) opened a dress department that catered to the tastes of the Aesthetic movement. This Liberty gown, with its subtle colours, naturalistic pomegranate and sunflower motif and loose, medieval styling is a typical example of Aesthetic dress.

OTHER COLLECTIONS
AUSTRALIA Powerhouse Museum, Sydney
AUSTRIA Austrian Museum of Applied Arts, Vienna
ENGLAND Ferens Art Gallery, Hull
FRANCE Musée de la Mode et du Costume de la Ville de Paris, Palais Galliéra, Paris; Musée de la Mode et du Textile, Louvre, Paris
HUNGARY Museum of Applied Arts, Budapest
US The Fashion Institute of Design and Merchandising, Los Angeles, California; Ohio State University Historic Costume and Textiles Collection, Columbus, Ohio; Wisconsin Historical Museum, Madison, Wisconsin

Naturalism; Pre-Raphaelitism; Rationalism;
New Romanticism

Baroque; Rococo;
Belle Epoque

The Rational Dress Society was formed in London in 1881 by Viscountess Harberton and Emily M King with the intention of revolutionising fashion for women. Appalled by the severe health risks posed to women by the highly restrictive and weighty outfits in fashion at the time, the society instead promoted comfortable, practical and lightweight alternatives.

DR GUSTAV JAEGER (1832–1917); **VISCOUNTESS HARBERTON** (1843–1911); **EMILY M KING** (unavailable); **GEORGE BERNARD SHAW** (1856–1950)

health; comfort; practicality; cycling; utility

Aside from the brief return to fluid Neoclassical styles at the beginning of the century, fashion's predilection for the corset had been persistent throughout the 1800s (and for centuries before). Deeply uncomfortable, unhygienic and highly restrictive, the corset inflicted, according to contemporary medical reports, a catalogue of unpleasant and sometimes dangerous side effects upon the wearer. These included crushed internal organs, punctured lungs and kidneys caused by broken ribs, severely reduced lung capacity, miscarriage, skin complaints and bad breath caused by poor digestion. Not quite as perilous but no less restrictive, the fashions for excessively weighty outfits of huge crinolines or cumbersome bustles, stiff fabrics and high heels also conspired to limit the comfort and freedom of women.

Motivated therefore by quite reasonable concerns for women's well-being, the Rational Dress Society was formed in London in 1881 by Viscountess Harberton and Mrs Emily M King, both outspoken campaigners for women's rights. The newly formed society did not promote an evolution, but rather a revolution in dress, and a radical manifesto, published in its own gazette, set out the aims of the organisation. It stated: 'The Rational Dress Society protests against the introduction of any fashion dress that either deforms the figure, impedes the movement of the body, or in any way tends to injure health', before going on to list specific 'outlawed' items. In 1884 the International Health Exhibition of London, or the 'Healtheries' as it was nicknamed, provided a platform for the Rational Dress Society and devoted a section to sanitary clothing for women. Viscountess Harberton displayed a modest divided skirt – what we now recognise as

culottes – and attracted hugely positive attention.

Analogous to the tenets of Rational dress reform were the theories of Dr Gustav Jaeger, an eminent German zoologist. Using his own transformation from sickly to healthy via the adoption of sanitary dress as evidence, he advocated that only yarns derived from animal sources (wool, cashmere) be worn next to the skin. Highly prescriptive, he issued an ominous warning that wearing yarns (such as linen) from plant sources would be comparable to inhaling poison because 'dead vegetable fibres absorbed dangerous vapours when cold and emitted them when warmed by the body thus poisoning the surrounding air'. The fact that this was nonsense did not inhibit his success nor the enthusiasm of his supporters.

Sir (John) Bernard Partridge, *George Bernard Shaw,* **1894. Watercolour; National Portrait Gallery, London, England** Having vigorously promoted the health benefits of wearing wool and keen to capitalise on his renown, Dr Gustav Jaeger granted a license to open a British firm called Dr Jaeger's Sanitary Woollen System Co Ltd. The company promoted an all-in-one tunic and trousers that precluded the need for a tie and collar and thus conformed to Dr Jaeger's prescription for healthy dressing. This offering soon expanded and, by the turn of the century, Jaeger was a purveyor of fine woollen clothing for both men and women, finding popularity with, most famously, Oscar Wilde and George Bernard Shaw.

← **Jacket and bloomers,** *c* **1895. Kyoto Costume Institute, Kyoto, Japan** The immense popularity of cycling as a leisure pursuit for women necessitated the adoption of a divided skirt or bifurcated knickerbocker, similar to those advocated by early (and much ridiculed) dress reformer Amelia Jenks Bloomer. Indeed the contemporary enthusiasm for all manner of outdoor sports demanded a rational approach to dress that was fit for purpose.

OTHER COLLECTIONS AUSTRALIA Powerhouse Museum, Sydney **ENGLAND** Gallery of Costume, Platt Hall, Manchester **US** Ohio State University Historic Costume and Textiles Collection, Columbus, Ohio

Bloomerism; Aestheticism; Utility; Return to Classics

Romanticism; Belle Epoque; The New Look

Closely related to Pre-Raphaelitism, the Arts and Crafts Movement was motivated by both social and aesthetic concerns. Disillusioned with the dehumanising effects of industrialisation and mass production, the utopian movement was dedicated to the revival and development of traditional craftsmanship. Originating in England, the tenets of the movement were adopted by various groups internationally and found expression in textiles, decorative arts and architecture during the late 19th century and early 20th century.

JOHN RUSKIN (1819–1900); WILLIAM MORRIS (1834–96); CHARLES ROBERT ASHBEE (1863–1942); ALEXANDER FISHER (1864–1936); JESSIE NEWBERY (1864–1948); JOHN PAUL COOPER (1869–1933); JOSEF HOFFMANN (1870–1956); JESSIE M KING (1875–1949)

Pre-Raphaelites; Gothic Revival; utopian; tradition; craftsmanship; truth to materials; Limoges

John Ruskin and William Morris were the founding fathers of the Arts and Crafts Movement. Appalled by the rapid industrialisation and consequent urban misery of the Victorian era and offended by the shoddy quality and ugliness of mass-produced goods, both were vigorous in their promotion of design integrity and traditional handicrafts.

Members of the Arts and Crafts Movement adopted a broadly recognisable clothing style that conveyed their principles: truth to materials, simple forms, revival of domestic traditions and natural motifs. For women, clothing was either home-made or produced in a small commercial studio, and crafted from natural and simple materials. It took its inspiration from Renaissance and medieval art, and comprised loose-fitting and smocked garments that evoked rural simplicity and could be layered to produce a linear and 'free' silhouette. Colours were derived from vegetable dyes and were rich but muted, and embroidery was used to create decorative detail, usually of flowers or other natural motifs. Gowns in the Arts and Crafts style could be purchased from London department store Liberty and Co, and many Paris couture houses adopted stylistic details (if not the ethos) associated with the movement

For men, the adoption of clothing more commonly associated with the working man was expressive of a sympathy with and concerns for his diminished status in an industrialised world, and showed respect for his supposedly noble relationship to the means of production. Others adopted a style closely related to that of the Aesthetic movement.

The design and production of jewellery in which value was given to technique and craftsmanship over material was a key branch of the Arts and Crafts Movement. Semi-precious (and relatively cheap) stones were used alongside the revived Limoges technique of translucent enamelling and obviously hammered silverwork. Designs took their stylistic cues from nature, mythology, Celtic legend and Renaissance and medieval art. Exemplars of Arts and Crafts jewellery included Alexander Fisher, John Paul Cooper and Jessie M King, as well as key Arts and Crafts figure Charles Robert Ashbee.

Although ostensibly concerned with the plight of the common man, the Arts and Crafts Movement was deeply anachronistic and much of its rhetoric was based on a romanticised, outmoded and privileged viewpoint. The goods they produced, the ideals they espoused and the style they promoted was beyond the means of (and probably of little concern to) those they sought to enfranchise.

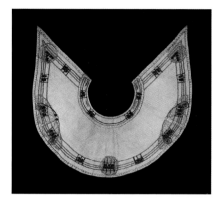

↑ Jessie Newbery, Embroidered collar, *c* 1900.
Victoria and Albert Museum, London, England
Jessie Newbery was a pioneering and inspirational member of the Glasgow Arts and Crafts Movement. Her work utilised simple and unrefined fabrics such as flannel and, although her designs were almost naive in their bold simplicity, Newbery was evangelical about quality craftsmanship. Her own mode of dress was influenced by peasant and Renaissance art and was crafted entirely by hand with layered, tunic-like robes,

OTHER COLLECTIONS
AUSTRIA Austrian Museum of Applied Arts, Vienna
CZECH REPUBLIC Museum of Decorative Arts, Prague
ENGLAND Birmingham Museum and Art Gallery, Birmingham; The William Morris Gallery, London
FINLAND Finnish National Gallery, Helsinki; Craft Museum of Finland, Jyväskylä
GERMANY Institut Mathildenhöhe, Darmstadt
HUNGARY Museum of Applied Arts, Budapest; Gödöllo Municipal Museum, Gödöllo
SCOTLAND Hunterian Museum and Art Gallery, University of Glasgow; National Museum of Scotland, Edinburgh
SWEDEN Nationalmuseum, Stockholm
US Museum of Fine Arts, Boston, Massachusetts; National Museum of American History, Smithsonian Institution, Washington DC

Wiener Werkstätte, Afternoon dress, 1917.
Los Angeles County Museum of Art, Los Angeles, California, US
Although the Arts and Crafts Movement was founded in the UK it had a palpable impact on the decorative arts in the US, Japan and Europe. Founded in 1903 by Josef Hoffmann, the Viennese Weiner Werkstätte (literally, Vienna Workshop) was influenced by John Ruskin's and William Morris' credo of simple functionality and quality craftsmanship, but rejected the social reform aspects of the British movement. Instead Hoffmann strove to create beautiful quality designs for a discerning clientele. Evolving out of the hand-painted and hand-printed textiles they had been producing for many years, fashion became a key department of Weiner Werkstätte, and a workshop dedicated to its production was created in 1910. Fashioned from hand-embroidered silk, this dress produced in 1917 displays characteristics of reform dress and the revival of the classical style that was also fashionable in Paris and London at the time.

 Bloomerism; Aestheticism; Rationalism

 Restorationism; Mass Productionism; Space Ageism

3

Introduction

⊙ During the 20th century, fashion underwent a radical and rapid transformation. What at the beginning of the era had been a luxury accessible to only an affluent minority transformed into a relatively democratic, pluralistic and fast-moving system communicated to, and participated in by the masses.

◑ mass production; Modernism; Postmodernism; democratisation; mass communication; pluralism;

● For the first 14 years of the 20th century, fashion continued in a manner that did not distinguish it greatly from that of the 1800s. Rigid social structures that ensured fashion was the privilege of the aristocracy were upheld; Paris and the dictates of the Haute-Couture industry still defined what it meant to be fashionable, and clothing was still not produced on a scale that made it an accessible or affordable prospect for the masses.

It was the First World War and its catastrophic impact that created a real dividing point between the centuries and, for a traumatised world, nostalgia was rejected in favour of Modernism and progress.

The full mechanisation of the clothing industry began to take place after the war. Clothing and textiles factories were forced to invest in appropriate machinery when they were deployed to make standardised army uniforms. Thus the postwar consumer benefited from a refined and more efficient industry better able to produce affordable ready-to-wear clothing. The Second World War provided another great catalyst for the advancement of quality, mass-produced clothing with the introduction of the Utility scheme. As well as being necessary, this brought numerous benefits to both the clothing industry and the general public such as quality, value and standardised sizes.

The 1960s ushered in the era of disposable and fast-moving fashions and by the close of the 20th century the manufacture of most types of fashion had become rapid and truly pluralistic; clothes were now available in numerous outlets at a wide range of prices and in any number of styles.

The 20th century also became an era of mass media and communication. The number and type of fashion journals increased and the use of fashion photographs began to supplant the use of illustrations. Once introduced their impact was great and they provided a portal for many into the rarefied world of Paris and London fashions as well as contributing to the increased rapidity with which fashion could cross over from the Haute-Couture salon to the mass market.

Motion pictures exerted a huge influence upon fashion from the 1930s. The costumes, hairstyles and make-up worn by Hollywood stars were widely disseminated and the studios were quick to install commercial frameworks that

→ Cecil Beaton, *Twiggy*, 1967.
The Cecil Beaton Studio Archive, Sotheby's, London, England
Twiggy (Lesley Hornby), a model from East London, personified the liberated, fast-paced and resolutely youth-oriented fashion of the 1960s. She shot to fame in 1966 at the age of 16 after being named 'Face of the Year' by the *Daily Express* newspaper.

could capitalise on this fascination with star style.

Mass media continued to evolve through the century. No longer was fashion communicated to the passive masses by a powerful elite. Magazines, television programmes and Internet sites existed that were run by, and catered to, all sectors of society.

Subcultures, which came to the attention of the alarmed mainstream in the 1950s with the Teddy boys, have at various points in the second half of the 20th century offered both an alternative to and inspiration for mainstream fashion. By the close of the century the process whereby fashion trickled down to the masses from the upper echelons of society had all but broken down.

After the 1960s and the ubiquity of the mini skirt, there was rarely one fashion that dominated above all others. Fashion began to display the characteristics of Postmodernism and became a fast-moving, heterogeneous, culturally non-specific, democratic and intertextual blend of high and low culture. No longer could we talk of one fashion, but instead had the choice of many.

Although Paris continued to dominate world fashion during the 20th century its position as the undisputed arbiter of style was successfully challenged by a series of new fashion capitals: New York, London and Milan.

From the 1950s, New York fashion became synonymous with unpretentious clean lines and functionality. In the 1970s, Milan established itself as a credible alternative to the hegemony of Paris. Taking advantage of both its sophisticated commercial infrastructure and a renaissance in the Italian textile industry, Milan flourished as a fashion capital. Krizia

and Missoni were at the vanguard of this. London, which for centuries had been venerated for its world-class tailoring, acquired a name for its youthful and irreverent fashion in the 1960s, and by the end of the century had developed a reputation as the home of the experimental and the exciting.

Although the hundred years from 1900 to 1999 bore witness to an almost unquantifiable number of designers and trends, it is possible to distinguish the names that have had a greater impact upon 20th-century fashion than any others. These include Paul Poiret, Madeleine Vionnet, Elsa Schiaparelli, Coco Chanel, Cristobal Balenciaga, Christian Dior, Mary Quant, Yves Saint Laurent, Vivienne Westwood, Giorgio Armani and Martin Margiela.

← **Elsa Schiaparelli, Evening dress with printed fabric designed by Salvador Dalí, Philadelphia Museum of Art, Philadelphia, Pennsylvania, 1930s**
The collaborative work of Elsa Schiaparelli and Salvador Dalí is one of the greatest instances of partnership between a designer and an artist. The fabric of this gown was designed by Dalí and is a trompe l'oeil depiction of torn animal flesh on silk crepe, influenced by his painting *Three Young Surrealist Women Holding in Their Arms the Skins of an Orchestra* of 1936.

KEY COLLECTIONS
AUSTRALIA National Gallery of Victoria, Melbourne, Victoria; Powerhouse Museum, Sydney
AUSTRIA Modesammlung des Historischen Museums, Vienna
BELGIUM Mode Museum, Antwerp
CANADA Costume Museum of Canada, Winnipeg
ENGLAND Fashion Museum, Bath; Museum of London, London; Victoria and Albert Museum, London
FRANCE Musée de la Mode et du Costume de la Ville de Paris, Palais Galliéra, Paris; Musée de la Mode et du Textile, Louvre, Paris
ITALY Galleria del Costume, Palazzo Pitti, Florence
JAPAN Kobe Fashion Museum, Kobe; Kyoto Costume Institute, Kyoto
NORTHERN IRELAND Ulster Museum, Belfast

Belle Epoque

Belle Epoque (1895–1914), literally translated as 'the Beautiful Era', was a golden period for the upper classes and this was reflected in the ostentatious clothing and lifestyles of the privileged few. Women wore opulent and romantic clothing, and the silhouette, created using corsetry, was that of an S-bend. The First World War swept away these impractical and elitist fashions to usher in a new era of Modernism.

QUEEN ALEXANDRA (1824–1925); EDWARD VII (1841–1910); LUCILE, LADY DUFF GORDON (1863–1935); CHARLES DANA GIBSON (1867–1944)

opulence; leisure; pouter pigeon; S-bend; frou-frou; tailor-made; Gibson Girl

The period from 1895–1914, known as the Belle Epoque in France, was distinguished by its splendour and opulence. Although ostensibly a fashion of the 20th century, the Belle Epoque was resolutely nostalgic and was arguably the swansong of the leisured upper classes.

Distinguished from her Victorian predecessor by a relatively narrow silhouette and increased physical stature, the Edwardian woman displayed a full 'pouter pigeon' bust with hips thrust back to create an extraordinary S-bend or 'kangaroo stance' figure. This was achieved with the use of the so-called 'health' corset which, although intended to reduce pressure on the diaphragm and follow the natural contours of the female form, succeeded only in creating a rigid and unnatural contortion.

Conversely, atop this rigid underpinning clothes took on an excessively romantic fluidity. Skirts fell from narrow hips towards the floor in a cascading bell shape; silk chiffon, crêpe de Chine, mousseline de soie and tulle were the favoured fabrics; colours were light, dreamlike and usually pastel in tone; and trimmings of ruffles, feathers, embroidery and, in particular, lace were used in abundance to create a frilly, or frou-frou, appearance. Particular cachet was given to Paris creations by Charles Frederick Worth, Callot Souers, Jeanne Paquin and Jacques Doucet. However, London was also establishing itself as an important and credible fashion city, aided by the patronage of the influential Queen Alexandra, wife of Edward VII. Lucile, Lady Duff Gordon was one of the finest and most important couturiers in Edwardian London.

For men, the relative restraint of their outfits provided a context in which the women could shine. Even though for formal occasions top hat and frock coat were required, the lounge suit was becoming more prevalent, trousers became narrower and shorter, faces were increasingly clean shaven, and hats, particularly the homburg and the straw boater, also experienced popularity. High enveloping collars mirrored the female fashion for boned lace collars.

Enjoyment of these fashions was dependent upon wealth and social status and as such was restricted to the upper classes and the newly created nouveaux riche. The expense of the garments and their impracticality rendered them wholly unsuitable for the vast majority. However, some styles did filter down which meant women of limited means could enjoy developments in the ready-to-wear market. The 'tailor-made', a suit that first found popularity in the UK in the 1890s, became popular with the middle classes and women going out to work. This was the only nod to Modernism in an era defined by nostalgia.

Travelling gown of bodice and skirt, 1905.
Victoria and Albert Museum, London, England
Hats were integral to the Edwardian silhouette and became excessively wide and cumbersome. They were fully decorated with feathers, flowers and sometimes arrangements of fruit, and hairstyles were full, elaborate and were often achieved with the addition of hairpieces and pads around which the hair was styled.

Charles Dana Gibson, *Scribners for June*, sketch, c 1898
The Gibson Girl was the creation of American illustrator Charles Dana Gibson and came to epitomise fashion, beauty and social success at the turn of the 20th century. His depictions of the beautiful, enlightened and spirited 'New Woman' set a huge trend for a tall, small-waisted silhouette bedecked in high-necked blouses and gored, tailored skirts.

OTHER COLLECTIONS
FRANCE Musée de la Mode et du Textile, Louvre, Paris
ITALY Galleria del Costume, Palazzo Pitti, Florence
JAPAN Kyoto Costume Institute, Kyoto
SOUTH AFRICA Bernberg Museum of Costume, Johannesburg
US Arizona Costume Museum, Phoenix Art Museum, Phoenix, Arizona; The Costume Institute, Metropolitan Museum of Art, New York; Los Angeles County Museum of Art, Los Angeles, California

Dandyism; Romanticism; The Birth of Haute Couture; The New Look

Mass Productionism; Modernism; British Boutique Movement; Japanese Avante-Gardism

Empire Revivalism

Towards the end of the 1910s, as the Belle Epoque drew to a close, the dominant silhouette for women softened. The restrictive and artificial S-bend created by flat-fronted corsets gave way to a more linear style. This was a revival of the Empire line last in fashion from 1800 to 1814, which in turn had been a revival of the classical lines worn by the ancient Greeks and Romans.

MADAME RÉCAMIER (1777–1849); JACQUES DOUCET (1853–1929); JEANNE PAQUIN (1869–1936); PAUL POIRET (1879–1944); PAUL IRIBE (1883–1935)

Directoire; Napoleonic; high waistline; Callot Soeurs; tea gown

Also known as Directoire or Madame Récamier (a famous beauty and fashion icon of the Napoleonic era), the revival of the Empire style saw the waistline move upwards from its natural position to settle just below the bust line, from where supple and soft materials would fall vertically to the ground. The change was not only aesthetic; women who had been bound into the extraordinarily unnatural S-bend corsets of the Edwardian era were able to experience relative comfort in a public setting for the first time.

Jeanne Paquin, Callot Souers, the House of Worth, Gustav Beer and Jacques Doucet provided designs that followed the new lines. But it was Paul Poiret, in keeping with his tendency for self-aggrandisement, who claimed he alone had freed women from their corsets. Although the revival of Empire styles shifted the emphasis from the waist to the bust, corsets of an evolved form were still in use. Women had not been freed from restrictive undergarments entirely and found they were obliged to use new tubular styles of corset.

The style was popular for evening wear and, in particular, tea gowns (or hostess gowns). These garments, which had been popular since the 1870s, were traditionally worn at home by society women as they received guests for afternoon tea, and their billowing style allowed a few hours of respite from binding corsetry.

There are a number of possible reasons for the revival of the Empire silhouette. In one sense reviving old fashions had become commonplace within modern fashion whereby there are a limited number of permutations available to the designer and consumers in need of change. Interestingly, though, the revival of Empire lines coincided with the style favoured by dress reformers who had campaigned for the liberation of women from restrictive and unhealthy clothing. For Poiret, a collector of non-Western garments and textiles, his designs were more likely to have been interpretations of the Greek chiton or based upon oriental costume than a conscious attempt at female emancipation.

Paul Iribe, Illustration of Paul Poiret gowns, 1908.
Victoria and Albert Museum, London, England
Paul Poiret worked closely with illustrators and artists throughout his career. These images by Paul Iribe were commissioned for a 1908 'catalogue' of Poiret's work entitled *Les Robes de Paul Poiret*. Iribe used the *pochoir* technique, hand-colouring of a printed black outline, to produce exquisite, bold and slightly abstract illustrations that perfectly represented the Empire line of Poiret's gowns. Only 250 of these books were published, but their impact was significant and they helped to redefine fashion illustration as well as making Iribe's reputation. The gown pictured on the right of the image is the Eugenie gown, an example of which can be found in the Musée de Mode et du Textile in the Louvre, Paris.

Callot Souers, Evening gown, 1909.
Drexel Historic Costume Collection, Drexel University, Philadelphia, Pennsylvania, US
Callot Soeurs (literally Callot Sisters) was a French couture house established in 1895. Run, as the name would suggest, by the four Callot sisters Regina, Marie, Marthe and Josephine, it was known for its elegant dresses with exotic detail and found favour with high society as well as being an inspiration to fellow designers. The sisters trained Madeleine Vionnet, one of the most venerated designers of the 20th century, who said of them: 'Without the example of the Callot sisters, I would have continued to make Fords. It is because of them that I have been able to make Rolls-Royces.'

OTHER COLLECTIONS
AUSTRIA Modesammlung de Historischen Museums, Vienna
BELGIUM Mode Museum, Antwerp
ENGLAND Brighton Museum and Art Gallery, Brighton
FRANCE Musée de la Mode et du Textile, Louvre, Paris
US The Museum at the Fashion Institute of Technology, New York

 Neoclassicism; Aestheticism; Arts and Crafts; Orientalism

 Romanticism; Deconstructionism; Football Casualism

Orientalism

 In its broadest sense, Orientalism is the fanciful depiction and adoption, in the West, of styles from the imagined Near, Middle and Far East. It had a palpable influence upon fashion in the years before the First World War and the designs of Paul Poiret best represent this aesthetic.

LEON BAKST (1866–1924); MARIANO FORTUNY (1871–1949); SERGE DIAGHILEV (1872–1929); RAOUL DUFY (1877–1953); PAUL POIRET (1879–1944)

Fauvism; exoticism; Ballet Russes; bold colours; lean silhouette; 'Thousand and Second Night'

Within the context of a wider and pervasive cultural trend, Orientalism was a dominant influence upon Paris fashion in the years leading up to the First World War. Distinguished by the use of vivid shades of orange, purple, black and jade green, bold prints and oriental embroidery upon a relatively lean silhouette, these fashions provided a sharp contrast to the frou-frou confections worn by women during the Belle Epoque.

This style had its origins within the arts. In Paris the 1905 exhibition by 'Les Fauves', which utilised violent and non-naturalistic colours ignited an interest in the exotic. However, the catalyst that transformed this trend into a craze was the 1910 production of *Scherezade* by Diaghilev's Ballet Russes. The sets and costumes designed by Leon Bakst transformed traditional ballet into a theatrical explosion which utlised dazzling colour within the revolutionary stage sets and extraordinary costumes. The effect on fashion was palpable.

The Parisian couturier Paul Poiret was at the centre of this, earning himself the monicker 'Pasha of Paris'. Although Poiret, a keen collector of ethnological textiles,

claimed to have been a forerunner of Bakst, there is no doubt that the success of the Ballet Russes crystallised his Orientalist vision. He designed harem pantaloons; models wore jewel-coloured turbans decorated with exotic plumes and heavy ornamentation; and rich fabrics were imported from the East. Poiret revived the use of luxurious Byzantine textiles and commissioned the Fauvist painter Raoul Dufy to design prints for him. He promoted a linear and somewhat tubular silhouette inspired by the Japanese kimono, the Greek chiton and the Middle Eastern kaftan, and boosted demand for these styles by hosting extravagant oriental costume balls-cum-fashion shows. The most famous of these, 'Thousand and Second Night', saw Poiret dressed as a sultan, his wife, muse and model Denise as the sultan's favourite, and all guests in compulsory 'oriental' fancy dress.

Poiret was not the only designer to embrace Orientalism in his collections; Callot Souers and Mariano Fortuny were also fine exponents of this style

Although he liked to portray himself as an artist, Poiret was, in the tradition of most successful couturiers, an astute businessman with a talent for self-promotion. When invited by prominent department stores to visit North America in 1913, he seized the opportunity to disseminate the oriental styles for which he and Paris had become renowned.

With his linear designs, Poiret paved the way for the *garçonne* style emblematic of Modernism and favoured by Chanel. However Chanel, ever the self-aggrandiser, was dismissive of his contribution to the style. After the war he did not temper his exoticism to accommodate the Modernist mood and his influence as a couturier waned.

← **Paul Poiret, 'Sorbet' evening dress, 1912. Victoria and Albert Museum, London, England** The Persian-inspired 'Sorbet' evening ensemble was an evolution of the 'minaret', or 'lampshade dress', worn by Poiret's wife and model Denise at the infamous 'Thousand and Second Night' costume ball. The tunic is wired to form a mini hoop over the long straight skirt and the beaded roses were a recurring motif in Poiret's designs.

→ **Mariano Fortuny, Pleated silk 'Delphos' dress, 1905–20. Museo del Traje, Madrid, Spain** Although Paul Poiret, erroneously, claimed to have freed women from the corset, other designers were simultaneously working towards a less restricted silhouette. Mariano Fortuny, an artist and self-taught dress designer, created the radical 'Delphos' gown in 1907, patented it in 1909 and continued to produce it in varying forms until his death in 1949. Influenced by the classical Greek chiton, the 'Delphos' was a minutely pleated silk dress that appeared to tumble over the natural contours of the body from the natural support of the shoulders. Venetian glass beads gave weight to the hem and provided decorative touches. Fortuny's exemplary pleating techniques have proved impossible to replicate and there were rumours that he used witchcraft to create them.

OTHER COLLECTIONS
CHILE Museo de la Moda, Santiago de Chile
FRANCE Musée de la Mode et du Costume de la Ville de Paris, Palais Galliéra, Paris
GERMANY Museum für Kunst und Gewerbe, Hamburg
ITALY Fortuny Museum, Museo Civice di Venezia, Venice
JAPAN Kyoto Costume Institute, Kyoto

 Aestheticism; Rationalism; Empire Revivalism; World Clothing; Rationalism

 Modernism; Utility; Space Ageism

Mass Productionism

 Although the Industrial Revolution had provided the rudimentary means by which fashions could be produced, distributed and retailed for mass consumption, and ready-made outfits for women had become popular with the middle classes and those going out to work from 1890, it was not until after the First World War that the ready-to-wear market gained real momentum.

LOU RITTER (dates unknown); **OLIVE O'NEILL** (dates unknown); **FREDERICK STARKE** (1904-88)

ready-to-wear; Dereta; Windsmoor; Dorville; mass market; copy; sweated labour; rayon

During the First World War, clothing factories and small workshops that had previously resisted expanding and developing their operations for a capricious womenswear market were deployed to produce standardised uniforms for the military. In the process they adopted new technology, refined their existing operations, increased their production capabilities and became a more cogent industry, better placed to provide the postwar world with affordable, quality, ready-to wear clothing.

The market was ready for these developments. Living costs were down, the number of salaried workers had increased and women (superficially at least) were enjoying newfound freedoms in the workplace and in their leisure time. The publication of magazines devoted to women and issues of health, beauty and fashion flourished, stimulating the appetite for new and affordable styles. Able to capitalise on this was a whole new industry devoted to providing ready-to-wear fashionable clothing at all levels of the market. Some couturiers, previously dedicated to the individual and handmade, diversified into ready-to-wear; the upper-middle-class lady could turn to the ready-made section of the department store or the newly founded high-quality 'wholesale couturiers' such as Dereta, Windsmoor and Dorville; and high-street retail chains such as Marks and Spencer provided relatively affordable ready-to-wear goods direct from the manufacturer.

Although fashionable garments were now available from a variety of sources at a multitude of prices, Paris was still the venerated source of trends. Styles that were born in the couture salon rapidly spread to

the purchase of ready-made clothing was beyond their means, however the decreasing costs of home sewing machines, the distribution of fashionable paper patterns and the ease with which the new fashions could be copied meant that fashion, which at the beginning of the century was the privilege of just a few, had become an accessible pleasure for nearly everyone.

← Hodson Shop Collection, Rayon dress, 1946.
Walsall Museum, Walsall, England
The search for an artificial alternative to expensive, labour-intensive and finitely available natural fibres began in the 19th century, but it was not until after the First World War that major breakthroughs took place. Rayon, made from wood cellulose chemically treated to produce yarns that were also known as artificial silk, transformed fashion's mass market and it was estimated that by 1938, 10 per cent of all fibre used in the production of clothing was synthetic. This had the greatest impact on fashions (and underwear) for the lower-middle and working classes and afforded them access to an improved range of fashionable clothing.

⇐ Hodson Shop Collection, Dress, 1927.
Walsall Museum, Walsall, England
This 'trickle down' and mass manufacture of fashions from Paris was stimulated by the ease with which the newly fashionable *garçonne* look (characterised by simple lines, pliable fabrics and minimal embellishment) could be copied. The hugely intricate, opulent and frou-frou nature of the clothing that had dominated the Belle Epoque period had precluded their multiple production.

the mass market. The reputable department stores and wholesale houses would purchase prototype garments, or toiles, direct from the couture houses with the express purpose of duplicating them; others, in what was a highly skilled job, would attend the salons, commit designs to memory and sketch them ready for copy. In addition, the publication of dedicated trade journals boomed.

Factory production of ready-to-wear clothing did not supplant the use of poorly paid hand work and the appallingly exploitative use of sweated labour, nor did it obviate the existence of the home-made clothing market. For a significant majority,

OTHER COLLECTIONS
ENGLAND Fashion Museum, Bath; Gallery of Costume, Platt Hall, Manchester; Worthing Museum and Art Gallery, Worthing; York Castle Museum, York
SCOTLAND National Museum of Costume, Shambellie House, Dumfries and Galloway
US The Costume Institute, Metropolitan Museum of Art, New York; Museum of the City of New York, New York; Museum of Art, Rhode Island School of Design, Providence, Rhode Island

 Industrialism; Utility; Globalism

 Baroque; The Birth of Haute Couture; The New Look

Modernism

After the First World War, Modernist fashions evolved and came to dominate the 1920s. Characterised by clean, simple lines, an androgynous silhouette and a lack of unnecessary adornment, Modernism sought to enhance the life of the wearer via its apparent rejection of unnatural restriction. Although as a fashion movement it had declined by 1929, the principles of Modernism have been hugely influential upon many fashions of the 20th and 21st centuries.

JEAN PATOU (1880–1936);
GABRIELLE 'COCO' CHANEL (1883–1971);
SONIA DELAUNAY (1885–1979);
CLAIRE McCARDELL (1905–58)

garçonne; cloche hat; chemise; sportswear; geometric; 'Poverty de Luxe; utopian

Modernism is an umbrella term for a number of movements united in their rejection of historicism during the early 20th century. Modernists embraced progress and sought to enhance human experience of the modern age by breaking with the past. Fashion was a key branch of Modernism and widely adopted its principles after the First World War.

Restrained and linear, Modernist fashion was the antithesis of the cumbersome garments popular during the Belle Epoque. This new and androgynous style was christened the garçonne look and dominated fashion until 1929. Hemlines were raised significantly, peaking in 1926 at just below the knee; waistlines dropped towards the hips; hair was bobbed, shingled or even cropped; the hugely popular bell-shaped, brimless cloche hats were pulled down; and the ubiquitous chemise dress hung from the shoulders to create a straight and somewhat tubular silhouette. In addition, new comfortable, fluid fabrics in a neutral palette of navy, black, beige and grey were utilised. Make-up enjoyed huge popularity and was used to temper the androgyny and enhance femininity. The designs of Coco Chanel and Jean Patou epitomise this period. In his use of sportswear and geometric shapes, Patou exemplified Modernism. However, it is Chanel's legacy that has proved enduring. She is credited with introducing the 'little black dress' and promoting the principle of simplicity as elegance. Her modest designs, stripped of decoration, neutral in colour and simple in shape were christened 'Poverty de Luxe'.

In keeping with the spirit of Modernism, and aided by the development of rayon and the simple shapes of the garments, rapid dissemination of styles was made possible. What was shown in the couture salons was soon readily available to the mass market via copy houses or paper patterns.

Although Modernism was utopian and the simple, sports-influenced lines of the *garçonne* look suggested physical liberation, this was paradoxical. The new fashion demanded a radical shift in the ideal female form and women endeavoured to become lithe and youthful with a flat bust, no hips and a childlike slenderness. Corsets were replaced by roll-on, reinforced 'flatteners' and dieting was vigorously promoted as the best way to achieve a fashionable physique. Pills, potions, extreme and faddish exercise as well as restricted diets were promoted to aid women in their quest for 'serpentine slimness'.

Ostensibly, Modernism waned in 1929, but as a clothing tradition its principles have continued to influence the fashion designers of the 20th and 21st centuries. In particular, the American designer Claire McCardell, with her simple and elegant sports-inspired clothing designs of the 1930s, 1940s and 1950s (including leggings and ballet slippers as street wear), urged women towards the freedom and flexibility they enjoy today.

← Gabrielle 'Coco' Chanel, Day suit, c1928. Kyoto Costume Institute, Kyoto, Japan

The combination of cardigan jacket, sweater and skirt has become a classic that still constitutes the archetypal Chanel look. This example in black wool crêpe is shown with a white wool jersey sweater. Chanel hugely admired the fluidity of jersey, which was previously only used for undergarments, and her house became synonymous with the fabric. She would go on to open a factory dedicated to its production.

← Gabrielle 'Coco' Chanel, Evening ensemble, 1925. The Costume Institute, Metropolitan Museum of Art, New York, US

Although she did not invent it (its evolution cannot be accredited to one designer) Chanel claimed authorship for the perennially elegant 'little black dress'. This claim served her well and in the October 1926 issue of American *Vogue* it was announced that Chanel's design was comparable to the perfect simplicity, functionality and popularity of the Model T Ford car – it would be, they claimed, 'the frock that all the world will wear'.

OTHER COLLECTIONS
AUSTRIA Wien Museum, Vienna
ENGLAND Fashion Museum, Bath; Victoria and Albert Museum, London
US Los Angeles County Museum of Art, Los Angeles, California

Utility; Minimalism; Return to Classics

Rococo; Belle Epoque; Victorian Revivalism; The New Look

◔ Hollywood was a major influence on the fashions of the 1930s. Costumes were central to a film's success and vast sums were spent on the wardrobes of the female stars. Hollywood style was pluralistic. It was just as well represented by the escapist, sultry, glamorous style of Greta Garbo and Jean Harlow as it was by the more sporty and casual look of Katharine Hepburn.

● SAMUEL GOLDWYN (1879–1974); TRAVIS BANTON (1894–1958); ORRY KELLY (1897–1964); EDITH HEAD (1897–1981); GILBERT ADRIAN (1903–59)

◑ escapism; costume; fashion tie-in; Letty Lynton; emulation

● Hollywood exerted a strong influence on the fashions, hairstyles and make-up of the 1930s. Costumes became central to the success of a film, and women, according to Samuel Goldwyn, would visit the cinema 'one to see the pictures and stars: and two to see the latest in clothes'.

Cinema initially looked to Paris for sartorial direction, but this presented a dilemma as changes in fashion could render a film immediately out of date. Following a sudden drop in hemlines at the end of the 1920s, preventative measures were taken to ensure that Hollywood was never caught out again. Although some Paris couturiers (most notably Elsa Schiaparelli) formed close relationships with the film studios, Hollywood sought to find its own fashion niche.

Hollywood developed and promoted its own designers who became fashion leaders in their own right. Travis Banton and Edith Head at Paramount, Orry Kelly at Warner Brothers and Adrian at MGM were among the most successful.

The relationship between Hollywood and the fashion industry was far from laissez-faire and a commercial framework was quickly constructed to capitalise on the lucrative fascination with the style of the stars. Fashion 'tie-ins' whereby studios would promote paper patterns or ready-to-wear copies of popular outfits were common. Magazines such as *Women's Filmfair* and *Film Fashionland,* dedicated to replicating the styles on screen, also became popular.

The most referenced dress of the era is the Letty Lynton gown worn by Joan Crawford in the 1932 film of the same name. Designed by Adrian, it was a white cotton organdie gown with dramatic puffed sleeves that helped propel the nascent trend for shoulder pads already seen in the collections of Schiaparelli. Such was the impact of the dress that half a million copies were sold by Macy's department store in New York.

Hollywood's sartorial influence was not restricted to women. Men paid attention to the styles worn by the lead male stars. Cary Grant, Gary Cooper, Edward G Robinson and Ronald Coleman helped to reinforce the trend towards British tailoring and American leisure clothes, while two-tone brogues or 'co-respondent' shoes were popularised by Fred Astaire.

For those unable to purchase or make the outfits, hairstyles and make-up were an affordable way to mimic a favourite star. Greta Garbo's bobbed hair and Marlene Dietrich's arched eyebrows were widely copied, and Jean Harlow's platinum-blonde hair sparked a surge in sales of peroxide. Max Factor, the wigmaker and beautician employed by the studios, capitalised on this flourishing grooming industry by launching his own cosmetics line.

The influence of cinema has continued to affect design and fashion marketing to the present day. Faye Dunaway's berets in

Bonnie and Clyde (1967); the Ralph Lauren-designed wardrobe worn by Diane Keaton as the titular *Annie Hall* (1977); and the black cherry-red of Chanel Rouge Noir nail polish worn by Uma Thurman in *Pulp Fiction* (1994) all elicited widespread fashion emulation.

← **Busvine dress, *c* 1936.**
Victoria and Albert Museum, London, England
Hollywood's influence upon the clothing styles of the 1930s was immense. Animal print and African-inspired fashions enjoyed huge popularity on the back of the Tarzan movies and other fanciful depictions of African culture.

→ **Jeanne Lanvin, Evening dress, 1935. Victoria and Albert Museum, London, England**
Satin was a fabric much beloved of Hollywood costume designers in the 1920s and 1930s. In the 1920s when silent movies were the standard, satin was able to catch the light and convey character, and in the 1930s when the 'talkies' dominated, it was valued for both its beauty and its ability to not make any noise when the actresses moved.

OTHER COLLECTIONS
US The Costume Institute, Metropolitan Museum of Art, New York; Los Angeles County Museum of Art, Los Angeles, California

◉ Victorian Revivalism; Celebrity Consumerism; Globalism

◒ Pre-Raphaelitism; Existentialism; Deconstructionism

○ Fashion enjoyed a fruitful and reciprocal relationship with the Surrealist art movement (founded in 1924) based upon a shared propensity for fantasy and displacement. This was frequently evidenced within the realms of window display, fashion photography and advertising during the late 1930s. Elsa Schiaparelli was one of the few fashion designers to actively engage with Surrealism, collaborating with key artists including Salvador Dalí and Jean Cocteau.

○ JEAN COCTEAU (1889–1963); ELSA SCHIAPARELLI (1890–1973); ANDRÉ BRETON (1896–1966); SALVADOR DALÍ (1904–89); JEAN-CHARLES DE CASTELBAJAC (1949–); FRANCO MOSCHINO (1950–94)

○ the unconscious; juxtaposition; displacement; trompe l'oeil

● Surrealism was a confrontational and experimental art movement dedicated to revising contemporary definitions of reality. It was founded in Paris in October 1924 by the poet and artist André Breton with the publication of the first *Surrealist Manifesto*, a critique on the excessive rationalism and materialism of Western society. Influenced by Freudian psychoanalysis, the Surrealists sought to reveal the creative potential of the unconscious and would juxtapose images of the real and the imagined to disconcerting effect.

With their common inclination towards escapism and fantasy, Surrealism and fashion shared a natural affinity. Surrealist artists were fascinated with the paraphernalia attached to the fashion industry (mannequins in particular) and used fashion and clothing to represent the threshold between the conscious and unconscious mind. In turn, the fashion

industry made ready use of the Surrealist device of displacement – the placing of an object or image in an unfamiliar and jarring location – particularly within the realms of window display, photography and advertising during the late 1930s.

While Surrealism directly influenced the presentation of fashion, it was not evident in the work of many designers. The notable exception was Elsa Schiaparelli. Throughout her career Surrealism had a profound effect on her sensibilities and she readily collaborated with key Surrealist artists. Her success began with a series of hand-knitted sweaters employing the illusory technique of trompe l'oeil (deceiving the eye). What appeared to be decorative bows at the neck and wrist were in fact part of the knitting pattern.

It was not in the silhouettes that Schiaparelli displayed her tendency towards the surreal, but in the details. Buttons took on the form of circus acrobats, beetles,

→ **Elsa Schiaparelli, Lobster print dress, 1937. Philadelphia Museum of Art, Philadelphia, Pennsylvania, US**
The lobster was a recurring motif in the work of the Surrealists and in particular Salvador Dalí. Dalí created the fabric for this dress designed by Elsa Schiaparelli and later owned by Wallis Simpson. Although the lines of this dress conformed to contemporary fashions, the use of lobster and parsley print silk was considered outrageous. Dalí wished the dress to be splattered with mayonnaise when worn, but Schiaparelli demurred. For the male companion of the wearer of this dress, Dalí designed a dinner jacket covered with part-filled brandy glasses.

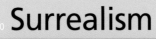

guitars, vegetables and lollipops; necklaces were made of flattened rhodoïd and adorned with aspirin tablets and insects; gloves came with painted nails; handbags lit up or played tunes when opened; and hats were presented as if they were shoes or, spectacularly, a lamb chop. Fabrics bore circus elephants, newspaper print and, in collaboration with Salvador Dalí, with whom Schiaparelli worked closely, a trompe l'oeil depiction of torn animal flesh on pale-grey silk crêpe (influenced by his painting *Three Young Surrealist Women Holding in Their Arms the Skins of an Orchestra,* 1936).

While Schiaparelli is closely associated with Surrealism, her prowess and inventiveness as a designer ensure that she is also revered as a fashion master and innovator. The wide-shouldered, narrow-waisted silhouette which dominated from the early 1930s until Dior's 'New Look' in 1947 has been accredited to her, and the introduction of mix-and-match separates, the use of themed collections, the backless swimsuit with built-in bra and the wrap dress can also all be traced back to Schiaparelli.

Surrealism as an art movement declined with the advent of the Second World War, but it has continued to exert a palpable influence on fashion and its representations to the present day. Designers as diverse as Karl Lagerfeld, Franco Moschino, Jean Charles de Caselbajac and Maison Martin Margiela have utilised the motifs of displacement and juxtaposition in their collections.

← **Elsa Schiaparelli, Embroidered linen jacket, motif designed by Jean Cocteau, 1937. Philadelphia Museum of Art, Philadelphia, Pennsylvania, US**
The magnificent detail of a woman's head in profile with her hair flowing down the sleeve of this evening jacket was embroidered by the House of Lesage and was translated from a drawing by the artist Jean Cocteau. Cocteau was a close friend of Schiaparelli's and she collaborated with him to supply the costumes for the actress Jany Holt in his play *Les Monstres Sacrés* (The Holy Terrors) in 1940 and for actress Maria Casarès in Robert Bresson's film *Les Dames du Bois de Boulogne* (The Ladies of the Park) in 1945.

OTHER COLLECTIONS
BELGIUM Mode Museum, Antwerp
ENGLAND Victoria and Albert Museum, London
FRANCE Musée de la Mode et du Textile, Louvre, Paris
JAPAN Kyoto Costume Institute, Kyoto
US Brooklyn Museum, New York; The Costume Institute, Metropolitan Museum of Art, New York; Drexel Historic Costume Collection, Drexel University, Philadelphia, Pennsylvania; The Museum at the Fashion Institute of Technology, New York

Hollywoodism; Punk; Deconstructionism; Postmodernism

Rationalism; Ritualism;
Mass Productionism

A nostalgic revival of romantic, full-skirted and small-waisted clothing styles occurred at the end of the 1930s as designers experimented with the neo-Victorian look. In response to the hardships of the Great Depression and the shadow cast by impending war, themes of escapism and fantasy dominated 1930s fashion, and this nostalgic and escapist fashion for Victorian-style clothing was gratefully received.

FRANZ XAVIER WINTERHALTER (1805–73); **GEORGE VI** (1895–1952); **ELIZABETH BOWES-LYON** (1900–2002); **NORMAN HARTNELL** (1901–79); **CECIL BEATON** (1904–80)

nostalgic revival; neo-Victorianism; escapism; costume balls; *Gone With the Wind*; *Little Women*

From the mid-1930s until the outbreak of the Second World War, couturiers experimented with a look reminiscent of Charles Frederick Worth's crinoline line: a full-skirted, small-waisted and voluptuous silhouette that had last been in favour at the end of the Victorian era and stood in direct contrast to the svelte and sinuous contours of contemporary fashions.

The source for the revival of this style was multifarious. In Paris the enthusiasm for elaborate and sumptuous costume balls served to both keep the couture industry solvent and resurrect styles last popular on the eve of the Franco-Prussian War. Hooped skirts and corsets became de rigueur on such occasions and the style filtered through to non-fancy dress.

The popularity of period Hollywood films also compounded the nostalgia for a Victorian silhouette. For formal occasions, particularly weddings, women sought to emulate the Walter Plunkett-designed

costumes worn by Vivien Leigh as Scarlett O'Hara in *Gone With the Wind* (1939) and Katharine Hepburn as Jo in *Little Women* (1933).

The key to the success of the Victorian Revival was its promotion by Queen Elizabeth II's mother, Elizabeth Bowes-Lyon, on a state visit to France in 1938. The London couturier Norman Hartnell was invited to design her wardrobe on this momentous occasion. Prompted by George VI, who wished his consort to emulate the elegance exemplified by Worth and his crinoline silhouette, Hartnell drew inspiration from Victorian portraits of European royalty by Franz Xavier Winterhalter. However, five days before the state visit, the Queen's mother, the Countess of Strathmore, died. Loathe to use mournful black and purple, Hartnell remade the entire collection in white, an outmoded mourning colour. The royal party was rapturously received and the popularity and adroit craftsmanship of Hartnell's neo-Victorian 'White Wardrobe' was duly noted by the French fashion industry and the style was emulated by Parisian couturiers. Even

Chanel, the staunch Modernist, displayed an inclination towards the romantic at this time. Elsa Schiaparelli, Mainbocher, Jean Patou and Cristobal Balenciaga also utilised Victorian motifs in their designs.

Interrupted by the Second World War and the need for frugality and practicality that it engendered, the lavish and romantic lines of Victorian Revivalism fell from favour before they had really taken hold. However, Victorian Revivalism can be viewed as a prescient glimpse at what was to become the defining silhouette of postwar fashion: the extreme hourglass of Christian Dior's misleadingly named 'New Look'.

Cecil Beaton, *Queen Elizabeth, the Queen Mother*, 1939. National Portrait Gallery, London, England

The 'White Wardrobe', designed for Queen Elizabeth by Norman Hartnell, was immortalised in a series of photographs by Cecil Beaton. Taken at the request of George VI, these portraits were key to the dissemination of the style. The composition, pose and outfit perfectly mimic the portraits of 19th-century European aristocracy by Franz Xavier Winterhalther, images which influenced the Victorian revival in the first place.

OTHER COLLECTIONS

The Birth of Haute Couture; Belle Epoque; Hollywoodism; The New Look

Aestheticism; Rationalism; Modernism; Utility; Minimalism

Cristobal Balenciaga, 'Infanta' gown, 1938–9. The Costume Institute, Metropolitan Museum of Art, New York, US

In contrast to his postwar linear designs, the 1939 'Infanta' gown designed by couturier Cristobal Balenciaga displays strong historical references. This full-skirted gown reflects the neo-Victorian focus of Paris at the time, but is in fact an interpretation of costumes worn at court by 17th-century Spanish princesses as depicted by the Spanish artist Diego Velázquez.

The Utility scheme was implemented during 1941 by the British Board of Trade to regulate the design, manufacture, pricing and quantity of clothing available to the general public. As befits clothing designed for frugality, the style was restrained and practical, characterised by squared padded shoulders, neat tailoring, boxy jackets, and skirts that exhibited only the regulated number of pleats. Though the war ended in 1945, the Utility scheme continued until 1952.

HUGH DALTON (1887–1962); **EDWARD MOLYNEUX** (1891–1974); **NORMAN HARTNELL** (1901–79); **DIGBY MORTON** (1906–83); **VICTOR STIEBEL** (1907–76)

Board of Trade; Incorporated Society of London Fashion Designers; austerity; rationing; Make Do and Mend

Befitting an initiative based on prudence, Utility clothing was tailored to produce a lean, spare silhouette. Boxy jackets, accentuated squared shoulders, lightly tailored waists, and skirts that were either straight or lightly pleated with hemlines that reached 18 inches (45.7 centimetres) from the floor. In 1942 the Making of Civilian Clothing (Restriction Orders) was passed to further regulate the criteria to which new clothing should conform. Buttons were limited, pockets restricted, seam and hem allowances were minimal, skirts were allowed only two box pleats or four knife pleats, and all embellishments were forbidden. Shoes, which were not regulated until June 1942, had to utilise cork, wood and raffia due to a rubber shortage, and the wedge, because of its longevity, became the dominant style for women. Those men not in military uniform found that they had to forego turn-ups on trousers, flaps on pockets, and braces and waistcoats. All clothing that conformed to the Utility scheme guidelines bore the logo CC41 (Civilian Clothing 1941).

In response to criticisms that Utility clothing was dictated by fashion, Labour politician Hugh Dalton invited leading members of the Incorporated Society of London Fashion Designers (ISLFD) to create prototype designs that could then go into mass production. Hardy Amies, Digby Morton, Edward Molyneux and Victor Stiebel were among the couturiers who participated. The remit was to design a stylish, basic wardrobe incorporating a modest day dress, coat and suit that conformed to the regulations and was suitable for all seasons. Thirty-two designs, graded into six sizes, were unveiled to the public with a fashion show in March 1942. *Vogue* heralded the designs with the proclamation: 'They're Beauties! They're Utilities!', and gave weight to the government propaganda that Utility did not mean the death of style.

Just as production and design were closely governed, so tight controls were placed on the purchase of clothes. In June 1941, the entire Utility scheme was augmented by rationing, whereby each person was entitled to 66 coupons per annum. This allowance permitted the acquisition of very few items so women had to be extremely thrifty and inventive if they were to maintain a wardrobe for themselves and their families.

Aware of this, the government launched the 'Make Do and Mend' initiative in 1943. Recommendations were made as to how to repair, rejuvenate or completely refashion old garments, and as the war progressed increasingly ingenious uses of available and unregulated fabrics were witnessed. Blackout material, furnishing fabrics, blankets and even Ordnance Survey Map linen allowed women to create their own fashions. New jumpers were knitted from unravelled wool, and wedding dresses and underwear were made from lace curtains.

The Second World War ended in September 1945, however British citizens were expected to carry on wearing cost-conscious and quality-minded clothing in the postwar world. In fact, severe shortages necessitated continued rationing until 1949 and the Utility scheme was not disbanded until 1952.

↑ Digby Morton, Utility suit, 1940s.
Victoria and Albert Museum, London, England
This is one of 32 prototypes designed by members of the Incorporated Society of London Fashion Designers in March 1942 and made available for production from October the same year. Although individual designs were not attributed to particular designers, this stylish grey herringbone suit and blouse with grosgrain bow bears the initials of Digby Morton.

Utility dress, 1940s. Gallery of Costume, Platt Hall, Manchester, England
Although the aim of the Utility scheme was to standardise clothing design and production, there still existed a hierarchy of quality and prices. At the cheaper end of the market clothing featured a high percentage of rayon and cotton as opposed to wool. This black rayon dress with waistcoat-style front displays the regulation four flared pleats and has only a very narrow cuff on its short sleeves. Ties at the waist hint that the dominant fashion silhouette of the late 1940s, Christian Dior's 'New Look', was already influencing the lines of Utility clothing.

OTHER COLLECTIONS
ENGLAND Bristol City Museum and Art Gallery, Bristol; Imperial War Museum, London; Museum of Childhood, London; York Castle Museum, York
US The Bard Graduate Center for Studies in the Decorative Arts, Design, and Culture, New York; Brooklyn Museum, New York

 Rationalism; Mass Productionism; Minimalism

 Rococo; Exoticism; Dandyism; The New Look; Glam

The 'New Look', launched in Paris in 1947, was a style of dress attributed to the couturier Christian Dior. Characterised by very full skirts, a hand-span waistline and gently sloping shoulders, it was a source of both controversy and wonder. Although initially considered shocking, the ultra-feminine and extravagant style became the dominant silhouette in womenswear for almost a decade.

CARMEL SNOW (1887–1961); CRISTOBAL BALENCIAGA (1895–1972); CHRISTIAN DIOR (1905–1957); JACQUES FATH (1912–54); PIERRE BALMAIN (1914–82)

'Corolle'; moulded; nostalgic revival; hourglass silhouette; Bar Suit

Christian Dior's 'New Look', the debut collection from his eponymous fashion label, was launched on the morning of 12 February 1947. Although originally entitled the 'Corolle' line because the skirts opened out like petals in bloom, it was almost instantly renamed the 'New Look' by Carmel Snow, then Editor-in-Chief of American *Harper's Bazaar*.

Lavish and feminine, it was the antithesis of the boxy, prudent and functional clothing worn during and immediately after the Second World War. Dior's creations were complex and moulded the body into an idealised female shape through the use of a rigid inner structure. He revived traditional techniques of construction using solid fabrics, the weight of which was reinforced with taffeta. The waist was narrow and tightly corseted, sloping shoulders emphasised rounded busts, hips were full and padded, skirts were deeply pleated and voluminous, and hemlines dropped towards the floor.

The reaction to this daring silhouette was unprecedented and the new fashion became a source of both wonder and controversy. Dior's creations, each of which used up to 25 yards (22.8 metres) of fabric, were condemned for insensitivity and scandalous extravagance in an era of rationing and severe postwar deprivation. Protests were voiced by governments and the public, and when Dior visited the US in September 1947 he was greeted with placards stating 'Burn Mr Dior' and 'Down with the New Look'. The ultra-constrictive style was also reviled by feminists who saw it as a step backwards in the emancipation of women.

However, the protests were useless and Dior's 'New Look' almost instantly re-established Paris as the commanding force in world fashion. Within a year it had become the dominant fashion in the Western world. The style was highly

→ Christian Dior, Bar Suit, 1947.
Victoria and Albert Museum, London, England
The Bar Suit was the first outfit from Christian Dior's first collection in spring 1947, and typifies the style of the 'New Look'. The jacket of natural Shantung silk is tightly fitted at the waist and slightly padded over the hips, and the black wool skirt is very full, deeply pleated and supported by a layered silk and tulle petticoat. This extravagant, restrictive and heavy ensemble was horrifying to those enduring the severe deprivation brought about by the Second World War.

commercial and (if you could afford the fabric) easy to copy. Magazines were full of advice on how best to replicate the look on a limited budget and which modifications could be made to existing clothing.

To call this the 'New Look', however, was something of a misnomer. The style was in fact a nostalgic revival of a bygone era of corseted waists, padded hips and narrow, sloping shoulders. Indeed, Dior's feminine revival had already been tentatively introduced in the late 1930s and again in 1946 by, most notably, Cristobal Balenciaga, Jacques Fath, Edward Molyneux and Pierre Balmain. Dior became the flag bearer for the movement rather than its originator, but all credit should be given to him for distilling and refining what was to become known as the 'New Look'.

During the 1950s the extreme hourglass silhouette championed by Dior was slowly rejected in favour of a less structured, more linear style. Indeed this tendency can be seen within his own collections from 1954 onwards, most notably the 'H', 'A' and 'Y' lines, so called to reflect the form they took on the body. In 1954 Coco Chanel came out of retirement prompted by, among other things, her revulsion at Dior's lack of regard for a woman's comfort or natural elegance. Within two years her simple cardigan suits, which initially seemed to be completely out of step with prevalent trends and were the antitheses of the 'New Look', had caught the public imagination and reflected a nascent mood in fashion. Likewise, Balenciaga was pioneering new shapes. His chemise, or sack dress, of 1957 gave a prescient glimpse at what was to become the most influential shape of the 1960s.

← Cristobal Balenciaga, Silk taffeta evening dress, c 1955. Victoria and Albert Museum, London, England

Although Dior and the 'New Look' grabbed the headlines, it is Cristobal Balenciaga who could arguably be described as the master couturier of this era. Renowned for his exemplary and innovative cutting techniques, Balenciaga worked with the female form and did not seek to restrict but to enhance it. His work during the period was characterised by two distinctive shapes. The first, as seen in this red silk taffeta evening dress from around 1955, was consistent with the fitted lines of the 'New Look'. The second was the prophetic barrel line, which was cut away from the body and anticipated the sack and trapeze silhouettes that came to dominate the 1960s.

OTHER COLLECTIONS
AUSTRALIA Powerhouse Museum, Sydney
CANADA Costume Museum of Canada, Winnipeg
JAPAN Kyoto Costume Institute, Kyoto
SPAIN Fundación Balenciaga, Guetaria; Museo del Traje, Madrid
US Chicago History Museum, Chicago, Illinois; Cornell Costume and Textile Collection, Cornell University, Ithaca, New York; The Costume Institute, Metropolitan Museum of Art, New York

Belle Epoque; Victorian Revivalism

Deconstructionism; Modernism; Rationalism; Space Ageism; Utility

New Edwardianism

A conscious attempt to reinstate the values of another era via the resurrection of its clothing styles, New Edwardianism was an elitist and nostalgic male fashion that was promoted by the tailors of Savile Row after the Second World War. It enjoyed limited appeal and, ironically, was appropriated by the UK's first postwar confrontational youth movement: the resolutely working-class Teddy boys.

CECIL BEATON (1904–80); **NEIL MUNRO 'BUNNY' ROGER** (1911–97); **NORMAN PARKINSON** (1913–90)

nostalgic; working-class appropriation; Youth Movement; Teddy boys

Deeply nostalgic, the New Edwardians cultivated a style that would not have looked out of place had they been transported back to the 1900s. The silhouette was one of spare, tight and restrained elegance. They wore fitted, narrow-shouldered, long-length jackets; coats with velvet-panelled collars were buttoned high; trousers were tight; slightly shrunken bowler hats sat atop the head; and silver-headed canes, Charvet ties and light leather gloves provided the finishing touches.

The look was immortalised by Norman Parkinson in the now iconic photograph *The New Mayfair Edwardians* (1950). Published in *Vogue* in

↓ Henry Grant, *Two men dressed in the 'Teddy boy' style*, 1953. Museum of London, London, England
These young men are dressed in the Teddy boy style, which blended Edwardian and American fashions. Through slicked, quiffed hair, draped jackets with velvet collars, narrow ties and peg trousers, the 'Teds' expressed their unwillingness to accept the drab clothing allotted to them in postwar Britain. By the mid-1950s, Teds had attracted a reputation, especially among the media, for violent and criminal behaviour.

April 1950, the image captures perfectly the key elements of New Edwardianism: elitism, restraint, militaristic leanings and Englishness. The style found favour among young officers of the Guards, the gentry and sartorial arbiters like Cecil Beaton and Neil Munro 'Bunny' Roger.

However, by 1953 the trajectory of this fashion took an ironic turn. What was supposed to be a style reserved for, and identifiable with, old-world values was adopted by the working-class and malevolent Teddy boys. In appropriating the garments of the New Edwardians, the Teddy boys undermined the elitist pretensions the clothes were meant to symbolise.

A 'Ted' (from the abbreviated form of Edward) prided himself on, and was instantly recognisable by, his appearance. A boxy-shouldered, thigh-length 'drape' jacket with velvet collar, four buttons and seamless 'full back' that fused classic Edwardian style with the wide-shouldered 'American' look; drainpipe trousers; thick crêpe-soled 'brothel creeper' or 'beetle crusher' shoes; and a shoestring tie known as a 'Slim Jim' would have marked him out. The suits were made by local tailors for the not inconsiderable sum of £20 to £30 when wages averaged £7 per week.

In what amounted to hysteria, the Teddy boys were demonised by the popular press. From 1954 to 1956, newspaper headlines warned the public of the immediate threat posed by the subculture.

As has become the familiar cycle with such fashions, just as it was gaining national and widespread popularity in 1956, the original Teddy boys were moving on. A hardcore remained and revivals have taken place, but the legacy of the Teddy boys was to leave the UK with a template that allowed working-class youths to assert themselves via appropriated sartorial codes.

→ **Carr, Sonn & Woor man's three-piece, single-breasted suit, 1951. Victoria and Albert Museum, London, England**
This three-piece New Edwardian outfit was a 1951 copy of a suit worn by Winston Churchill in a 1911 photograph. Mirroring the timing and retrospective focus of Christian Dior's 'New Look', New Edwardianism was an attempt to resurrect the unchallenged hegemony last enjoyed by the English upper-classes before the First World War. The bowler hat here is by Thomas & Stone, and dates from around 1960.

OTHER COLLECTIONS
ENGLAND Brighton Museum and Art Gallery, Brighton; Gallery of Costume, Platt Hall, Manchester; National Portrait Gallery, London

 Dandyism; Belle Epoque; Savile Row; Punk; Football Casualism

 Bloomerism; Rationalism; Utility; Space Ageism

Existentialism

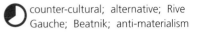
Usually educated, white and middle class, Existentialists rejected materialism and thus (theoretically) fashion. However, this anti-fashion stance became a trend all of its own and the uniform adopted eventually filtered into the fashion system. Oversized fisherman's sweaters, drainpipe trousers or jeans, turtleneck jumpers, undressed hair and duffle coats are all representative of the look.

COLIN MacINNES (1914–76); JACQUES ESTEREL (1918–74); JULIETTE GRÉCO (1927–); AUDREY HEPBURN (1929–93); BRIGITTE BARDOT (1934–); YVES SAINT LAURENT (1936–2008)

counter-cultural; alternative; Rive Gauche; Beatnik; anti-materialism

Existentialism was a disparate cultural movement that emerged in the late 1940s and persisted until the 1960s. United by a belief in the centrality of free will and the analysis of human existence, Existentialists were counter-cultural and provided an alternative to the mainstream while articulating a critique of the status quo.

Each country had its own take on, and name for, the Existentialist look. In France it was the Rive Gauche, or Left Bank, look

(named after the area in Paris where they congregated). This style was personified by the angst-ridden beauty of Juliette Gréco who wore her black hair long and undressed, and was clothed entirely in black. In the US they were the Beat generation and then the Beatniks, and stereotypically wore (for men) berets, goatee beards, chinos and black turtlenecks and (for women) black leotards, ballet pumps and oversized sweaters. In the UK the Existentialist movement fused the Rive Gauche and Beatnik looks and women wore duffle coats, opaque black or burgundy stockings, sloppy joe fisherman's sweaters, tight trousers or cropped jeans worn with flat sandals or ballet pumps; the style for men was similar. The novel *Absolute Beginners* by Colin MacInnes presents a fictional chronicle of this scene in London in 1958.

Simple, unstructured clothing also became emblematic of the anti-materialist stance of Existentialists. In 1956, Brigitte Bardot sensationally wore a pink gingham dress for her wedding to Jacques Charrier. Although a designer dress (by Jacques Esterel) for a celebrated film actress at the height of her career and expressive of her own sexy but ingénue image, it appears simple and unaffected and is representative of Bardot's own stance on anti-materialism.

Inspired by the style of the Left Bank, Yves Saint Laurent, while a designer for Christian Dior in 1960, presented a Beat collection. In what is now common practice, he had taken a street fashion and presented it as Haute Couture. The reaction was one of complete outrage and the attitude of his employers was clear when they did not contest his conscription to the French army later that year. Existentialism as expressed through clothing has become a standard fashion and persists in the counterculture as well as mainstream and high fashion.

← Ensemble, date unknown. Victoria and Albert Museum, London, England
Adopted as an anti-establishment counterpoint to the outfits worn by the mainstream in postwar America, this combination of sheepskin-lined leather jacket, plaid shirt layered over a white T-shirt, cotton chino-style trousers and army issue boots was a look favoured by the Beat writers Jack Kerouac and Neil Cassidy.

← Cecil Beaton, *Audrey Hepburn dressed in black*, 1954. Vintage bromide print; National Portrait Gallery, London
Hollywood provided its own take on the Rive Gauche look and in turn helped to popularise it as a mainstream fashion. Audrey Hepburn played an intellectual librarian in the film *Funny Face*. Fred Astaire, based on photographer Richard Avedon, 'spots' her and she becomes a model. This jazz scene shows Hepburn dressed head to toe in 'Existentialist' black. The look has become iconic and highly influential on clothing into the 21st century.

OTHER COLLECTIONS
ENGLAND Brighton Museum and Art Gallery, Brighton
FRANCE Musée de la Mode et du Textile, Louvre, Paris
US The Costume Institute, Metropolitan Museum of Art, New York

Punk; Japanese Avant-Gardeism; Deconstructionism

Baroque; Dandyism; Yuppieism

British Boutique Movement

TWF

◔ Part of both a cultural and retail revolution, the British Boutique Movement was a response to the demand for more affordable, fast-moving and youthful fashions in the early 1960s. In stark contrast to the existing department stores and fashion outlets that offered slow-changing fashions for a more mature clientele, the new boutiques stocked clothing designed specifically for the young and were run like clubs where the decor, music and shop assistants all contributed to the new shopping experience.

◑ **ALEXANDER PLUNKETT GREENE** (1932–90); **JOHN STEPHEN** (1934–2004); **MARY QUANT** (1934–); **BARBARA HULANICKI** (1936–); **JOHN BATES** (1938–); **SALLY TUFFIN** (1938–); **MARION FOALE** (1939–); **'OSSIE' CLARK** (1942–96); **JEFF BANKS** (1943–)

◑ youth explosion; teenager; Biba; disposable fashion; Bus Stop; Ginger Group; Carnaby Street; swinging sixties

● The explosion of youth fashions and the analogous emergence of the British Boutique Movement in the 1960s was a consequence of quite particular socioeconomic circumstances. Teenagers now made up a greater percentage of the population than ever before and most of them had substantially more disposable income than their parents ever had at the same age. In addition, a new generation of designers fresh from pioneering fashion design courses found themselves excluded from the hierarchical, ageist fashion system, so opted instead to open their own youth-relevant fashion boutiques.

These boutiques were the perfect expression of the (ostensibly) liberated 1960s and supplied affordable, throwaway fashions in an atmosphere that was more akin to a social club than a clothing store. Boutiques such as Bus Stop, Clobber, Miss Mouse, Quorum and Granny Takes a Trip were supplied by a new generation of talented designers like Marion Foale and Sally Tuffin, John Bates, Jeff Banks and Ossie Clark.

At the vanguard of this fashion revolution was Mary Quant. With her husband Alexander Plunkett Greene and business manager Archie McNair she opened Bazaar on the King's Road in 1955. This pioneering shop with its beautifully merchandised window displays, high turnover of affordable ready-to-wear stock and unstuffy atmosphere was frequented by an eclectic social mix all enticed by her easy-to-wear clothes in simple shapes and innovative materials. By 1963 Quant had gone into mass production with the Ginger Group range and put her distinctive daisy logo on a number of products including make-up, tights and shoes.

Barbara Hulanicki of Biba, probably the most fetishised and romaticised of the boutiques, peddled a markedly different style to Quant. Influenced by Art Deco and Art Nouveau as well as the excesses of Hollywood glamour, the clothes were a contrast to the bright, futuristic Pop styles that typified the era, particularly in the use of funereal 'auntie' colours like mulberry, bottle green, blueberry, rust and plum.

Credited with founding Carnaby Street as a fashion centre to rival the King's Road, John Stephen, a young Glaswegian fashion

designer and entrepreneur, did for menswear what Quant had done for women; he understood the need to show off and knew that young men did not want to dress like their fathers.

Although there were successful regional British boutiques and America had its own take on the movement, this was essentially a London-centric phenomenon. In April 1966 New York-based *Time* magazine announced this to the world in a cover story entitled 'London – the Swinging City', and the 1960s were christened with the moniker.

Now that London was the focus of the world's fashion gaze Paris, which had been the sartorial bellwether for over two centuries and had maintained a distance from and disdain for youth fashions when they first appeared in the 1950s, was forced to take notice. The response was the development of prêt-à-porter (ready-to-wear) fashions by couture designers, the explosion of mass licensing and a new wave of Parisian designers influenced by the youth quake in London.

Mary Quant, 'Quant Afoot' ankle boots, 1967. Victoria and Albert Museum, London, England
New synthetic materials were used by designers to create cutting-edge, youthful and sometimes futuristic designs during the 1960s. These plastic boots, designed by Mary Quant as part of the 'Quant Afoot' footwear range, are clear, and it is the interchangeable lining that provides the jolt of bright colour. The company logo, a stylised daisy, was moulded into the base of the heel so leaving a trail of flowery footprints should the wearer be walking in the rain or snow.

↓ **Mary Quant, Mini dress, 1967. Victoria and Albert Museum, London, England**
The mini skirt has become shorthand for 1960s female fashion and credited with its popularisation in the UK was Mary Quant. The almost wholesale adoption of this style (ranging from just above the knee to thigh high) was made possible when tights or pantyhose were developed and made available for sale, thus offering protection from both the elements and prying eyes.

OTHER COLLECTIONS
AUSTRIA Wien Museum, Vienna
BELGIUM Modemuseum, Hasselt; Mode Museum, Antwerp
ENGLAND Fashion Museum, Bath; Museum of London, London; Walker Art Gallery, Liverpool Museums, Liverpool; Worthing Museum and Art Gallery, Worthing
SPAIN Museo del Traje, Madrid
US Arizona Costume Institute, Phoenix Art Gallery, Phoenix, Arizona; Los Angeles County Museum of Art, Los Angeles, California; The Museum at the Fashion Institute of Technology, New York

◉ New Edwardianism; Glam Mass Productionism

◖ Neoclassicism; The Birth of Haute Couture; The Internet

added to the impression of a wardrobe engineered for the 'space age'. *Queen* magazine was the first to applaud his innovative, ultra-modern designs, having announced in the same year that clothes shown by established Paris couturiers were 'dreary', while Brigitte Bardot declared that 'Couture is for grannies'.

Traditional couture skills and textiles were matched with young, futuristic garments and synthetic materials in Courrèges' collection. The designs reflected the contemporary interest in space travel and science fiction. His 'moon girls' wore slim hipster trousers with short tunic dresses and jackets, or mini skirts with calf-length, square-toed boots in soft, white leather. Hats were large and helmet shaped, and opaque white sun goggles with slit lenses reinforced the Space Age theme. Strong clean shapes were based on simple trapeze lines for dresses and coats made up in white fabric. White dresses were trimmed with boldly coloured piping, and futuristic trouser suits were made in white and silver. Later collections introduced see-through and cut-out dresses.

Two other designers of the period were also utilising an innovative use of colour and texture, superb cut and skilful tailoring. By the early 1960s, Pierre Cardin was already widely influential, having defied the Chambre Syndicale de la Couture Parisienne with a mould-breaking ready-to-wear collection in 1959. Cardin's contribution to fashion's space race included a 1964 collection of clothing for men and women that incorporated rounded collars and polo-neck jerseys, short skirts, knitted catsuits, tight leather trousers, jumpsuits and helmet-shaped hats with moulded plastic visors.

After working with Courrèges from 1961, Emanuel Ungaro went on to open a studio

◕ Space Ageism takes its name from Paris designer Andre Courrèges' iconic 1964 collection that incorporated minimal styles, white fabrics and shiny or reflective modern synthetic materials. Accessories such as helmet-shaped bonnets and white kid or patent boots completed the look.

 PIERRE CARDIN (1922–); **ANDRÉ COURRÈGES** (1923–); **EMANUEL UNGARO** (1933–); **PACO RABANNE** (1934–)

 modern; futuristic; simple; bold

● André Courrèges jolted the fashion world when he presented his 'Space Age' collection in 1964, revolutionising women's fashion with trouser suits, and skirts several centimetres above the knee. The use of silver and white, vinyl trims, helmet-shaped bonnets and glossy boots

with his partner Sonja Knapp in 1965. Ungaro's range demonstrated his own take on young, futuristic fashion with brightly coloured coats and suits, shorts, A-line dresses, see-through lace dresses, thigh-high boots, over-the-knee socks and metallic garments. His collections featured new synthetic fabrics, as well as specially made textiles from Italian firm Nattier.

Traditional fashion rules continued to be broken in 1966, ultimately taking the most wearable ideas from Parisian couture to the high street. Transparent vinyl and brightly coloured PVC translated easily into snazzy rainwear, while materials with metallic finishes such as lurex were popular for evening wear. By contrast, Paco Rabanne's body jewellery was taken up only by an elite avant-garde.

Pierre Cardin, Man's ensemble from the 'Cosmos' collection, 1967. Victoria and Albert Museum, London, England
Inspired by science-fiction films for the big and small screens, this futuristic outfit from Cardin's 'Cosmos' range is reminiscent of *Star Trek* and *2001: A Space Odyssey*. Similar uniform-like outfits were made for men, women and children. For a radical change from a suit, shirt and tie, Cardin dressed his male cosmonaut in woollen jersey. The tunic features heavy zip fasteners and is worn with a shiny patent leather belt over a polo neck.

OTHER COLLECTIONS
AUSTRALIA National Gallery of Victoria, Melbourne
ENGLAND Fashion Museum, Bath; Gallery of Costume, Platt Hall, Manchester
FRANCE Musée de la Mode et du Textile, Louvre, Paris
JAPAN Kyoto Costume Institute, Kyoto
US The Costume Institute, Metropolitan Museum of Art, New York; Los Angeles County Museum of Art, Los Angeles, California; The Museum at the Fashion Institute of Technology, New York

Modernism; British Boutique Movement; Postmodernism

Bloomerism; Ritualism

↓ **Paco Rabanne, Chain-linked dress, 1967. Museo del Traje, Madrid, Spain**
Many designers and manufacturers experimented with shiny new modern materials. From 1966 Paco Rabanne produced innovative and sculptural chain-link dresses. Clients purchased a box of shaped plastic discs, which were then linked together with metal to make the chosen garment. Rabanne also designed Jane Fonda's wardrobe for the science-fiction movie *Barbarella* in 1968.

Defined by a stomping US rock-and-roll beat mixed with highly camp and stylised British showmanship, Glam (or Glitter as it was known in the US) was as much a visual movement as it was a musical genre. The first real youth style of the 1970s, it was defined by its theatricality, androgyny and, as the name would suggest, glamour. It was the antithesis of the hippy-dominated late 1960s and provided a perfect introduction to the fragmented, anything-goes fashions of the 1970s.

TERRY DE HAVILLAND (1938–); LEEE BLACK CHILDERS (1945–); KANSAI YAMAMOTO (1944–); BRYAN FERRY (1945–); MARC BOLAN (1947–77); DAVID BOWIE (1947–); JAYNE COUNTY (1947–); ANGIE BOWIE (1949–)

camp; Glitter; androgyny; glamour; Theatre of the Ridiculous

Clothing was integral to Glam and fashions quickly crossed over from stage to audience. The feather boas, glitter make-up, sequined jackets and satin pants of Marc Bolan; the hybrid of futurism with 1930s and 1940s Hollywood glamour as exhibited by Brian Ferry and Roxy Music; and the orange-dyed, feather-cut hair and tight jumpsuits of David Bowie all rapidly disseminated to create an eclectic look that was completely alien to any style culture that had come before it. Androgyny, glitter, metallic lamé, cropped satin bomber jackets, jumpsuits and platform boots, preferably made by Glam cobbler Terry

de Havilland, were all staple elements of Glam fashion.

The impact of David Bowie or, more specifically, his alter ego Ziggy Stardust, on the fashion-consciousness of the early 1970s cannot be overplayed. His bright-orange, feathered mullet hairstyle, shaved eyebrows, whited-out and painted face, extreme slenderness emphasised by the Kansai Yamamoto-designed costumes and vertiginous platform boots spawned thousands of Ziggy clones. The source of his look (and the catalyst for his transformation from winsome and folky to the polysexual and alien Ziggy) has been attributed to the influence of drag queens Jayne County and Leee Black Childers. Both part of the extreme New York scene that Andy Warhol presided over, they introduced Bowie to the sleazy, no-holds barred world of the Factory. While in New York in 1971, County and Childers acted as chaperone (significantly, introducing him to the subversive performance group Theatre of the Ridiculous, whose trademark was the use of glitter) while Bowie observed and absorbed. His wife Angie Bowie, although vilified by his obsessive fans, also played a vital role in his transformation, encouraging him to draw upon his proclivity for showmanship.

Glam's contemporaneous influence on US fashion was more limited. An Anglophile and music obsessive, Rodney Bingenheimer, introduced Glam to Los Angeles with the Rodney Bingenheimer's English Disco (1972–5). The club soon became the centre of the US Glitter (Glam) rock scene, playing host to Glitter rockers the New York Dolls and Iggy Pop. Outfits were a more sexualised version of British Glam.

Although Glam as both musical genre and fashion had faded by 1975, it has had a pervasive influence on fashion ever since. The highly sartorial New Romantic movement drew direct inspiration from its ethos and look.

← **Biba woman's gold lamé jacket, 1965–9. Victoria and Albert Museum, London, England**
Biba, the iconic London boutique founded in 1964, had a style that was very particular and quite distinct from its contemporaries. Influenced by the excesses of Art Nouveau and Art Deco as well as the glamour of 1930s Hollywood, the camp Biba style, especially from the late 1960s, had a marked impact upon the Glam aesthetic.

← **Terry de Havilland, Platform shoes, 1972. Walker Art Gallery, Liverpool, England**
Terry de Havilland was *the* Glam Rock cobbler and supplied footwear to most of the Glam rock fraternity. The son of an East London shoemaker, he popularised the three-tier wedge and made glorious snake- and crocodile-skin platforms for Marc Bolan, David Bowie and a coterie of 1970s stars. His shop, Cobblers to the World on London's King's Road, closed in 1979. However, after an extended break he relaunched his company in 2004.

OTHER COLLECTIONS
US Hard Rock Cafe, Orlando, Florida; Philadelphia Museum of Art, Philadelphia, Pennsylvania

 Restorationism; Aestheticism; New Romanticism

 The Birth of Haute Couture; Utility; Existentialism

Nostalgic Romanticism

 In contrast, and arguably in reaction to, the typically fast-moving, eclectic and synthetic styles of the 1970s there developed a trend that looked to an idealised version of the past for inspiration. Nostalgic Romanticism took its stylistic cues from the pastoral idylls of Victorian and Edwardian era Britain and found expression in simple smocked dresses and aprons in delicately printed cottons.

LAURA ASHLEY (1925–85); **RAYMOND 'OSSIE' CLARK** (1942–96); **RALPH LAUREN** (1939–); **CELIA BIRTWELL** (1941–)

idealised; smocking; pastoral idyll; innocence; prairie look

The 1970s trend for Nostalgic Romanticism was exemplified in the work of Laura Ashley. The tale of this woman and her business is an incongruous marriage of home-spun values and a tenacious business acumen. What began in the UK as a cottage industry in 1953 specialising in traditional country-print tea towels, napkins, place mats and aprons evolved into a phenomenally successful and hugely influential business that gained rapid momentum throughout the 1970s. One shop became a chain, which would go on to establish itself in the US, Canada, Australia and Continental Europe.

Following a similar style to Victorian and Edwardian era nightwear and everyday clothing, Laura Ashley's dresses evoked simpler times and presented an idealised version of pastoral innocence. Puffed 'leg o' mutton' sleeves; unsophisticated and cheap cottons either in virginal white or printed with sprigs and other delicate floral motifs; frilled hems, cuffs, and necklines sometimes created with the addition of machine-made lace; high, modest necklines; raised waistlines with pin-tuck pleats and smocking; and long tiered skirts were all typical components of the Laura Ashley look. The homely image was underlined by the marketing campaigns that presented improbable scenes of young, fresh-faced models photographed in rural landscapes carrying baskets of wild flowers.

In the US, Ralph Lauren, working with similar principles to Laura Ashley, produced collections inspired by the home-spun values and aesthetic of the early settlers in the American Midwest. The 'prairie look', which would become his leitmotif, was influenced by the styles sold in Sears and Roebuck catalogues of the 1880s and 1890s and featured ample use of gingham and simple calico cotton for petticoated dresses with ruffled hems and cuffs. Although reworked to appeal to a contemporary

Nostalgic Romanticism

market, Lauren's marketing and styling were deeply nostalgic for, and thus promoted, the 'traditional' American way of life.

Not all proponents of Nostalgic Romanticism presented quite such a wholesome image. The work of Raymond 'Ossie' Clark referenced and represented the glamour, hedonism and overt sexuality of late 1960s and early 1970s London. Whereas Laura Ashley and her designs have typically been defined as well marketed, conservative and middle class, Clark was an exceptionally gifted but volatile designer whose clothing was favoured by a much faster set. However, the sexuality of his designs was tempered by his romantic motifs and the use of exquisite and pretty chiffons designed by his then wife, Celia Birtwell. Cascades of ruffles, handkerchief hems, full sleeves and smocking were typical of his work in this era and were printed with trellises of flowers, stylised sprigs of daisies or naive interpretations of shooting stars.

Ossie Clark, Printed chiffon dress, 1970–71. Victoria and Albert Museum, London, England
One of Britain's most influential designers of the 1960s and 1970s, Ossie Clark presented a provocative take on the trend for Nostalgic Romanticism. Sheer fabrics and daringly plunging necklines were signature motifs, but the overt sexiness was tempered by his use of pretty and stylised textiles (in this example of hearts, poppies and feathers) designed by his collaborator and then wife Celia Birtwell. A contemporary fashion editor said of Clark's designs: 'His cut and Celia's prints were indivisible. They were delicate, divine and utterly desirable.'

↓ **Laura Ashley, Printed cotton day dress and straw hat, 1974. National Gallery of Victoria, Melbourne, Australia**
The Laura Ashley style was unashamedly pretty and was inspired by romantic ideas of Victorian and Edwardian pastoral idylls. Her collections tapped into the British love of country life and she enjoyed phenomenal commercial success, typically finding favour with a particularly middle-class and often urban consumer.

OTHER COLLECTIONS
AUSTRALIA Powerhouse Museum, Sydney
BELGIUM Mode Museum, Antwerp
ENGLAND Gallery of Costume, Platt Hall, Manchester; Warrington Museum and Art Gallery, Warrington
WALES Llanidloes Museum, Powys; Newtown Textile Museum, Powys; Powysland Museum, Welshpool, Powys
US The Costume Institute, Metropolitan Museum of Art, New York

Naturalism;
Neoclassicism;
Romanticism

Space Ageism;
Deconstuctionism;
Football Casualism

World Clothing

Heightened knowledge and appreciation of the dress worn by different cultures has influenced fashion, and throughout the mid- to late 1960s and early 1970s this became a pronounced trend as designers freely mixed influences from different cultures within their designs.

THEA PORTER (1927–2000); **YVES SAINT LAURENT** (1936–2008); **BILL GIBB** (1943–88)

multicultural; exotic; oriental; eclecticism; hippy trail; kaftan

Representations of the exotic have been a constant within fashion history. The adoption of the banyan by Western men of the 17th and 18th century; Charles Frederick Worth's use of chinoiserie-style printed silks in the 1880s; Paul Poiret's fantastical Orientalist garments and parties in the 1910s; and Chanel's version of a *roubachka* (a long belted blouse worn by Russian peasant women) made in lux crêpe de Chine in 1922 are all representative of fashion's enduring fascination with World Clothing traditions. From the late 1960s, the adoption of non-Western clothing traditions within the disparate sectors of designer, mainstream and counter-cultural fashion became a pronounced trend.

Throughout his career, Yves Saint Laurent deftly deployed various World Clothing traditions within his designs. The 1967 'African' collection was an uncompromising vision that broke with convention by utilising flax and raffia mixed with ebony, ivory, wood and glass bead embroidery within a Haute-Couture collection. Although these garments were wholly derived from African clothing and art traditions, Saint Laurent avoided parody by refusing to temper their ethnic origins in favour of a more palatable Western aesthetic. Continuing his cultural eclecticism, his 'Russian' collection for Autumn/Winter 1976, based on traditional Cossack clothing and influenced by the wildly dazzling Ballet Russes, was rich, sumptuous and culturally informed. Closely following this success was the 'Chinese Opera' collection for which he drew upon the romantic and ancient aspects of China. Running parallel to the cultural eclecticism displayed by the fashion industry was the rejection of modern values by the hippies and other counter-cultural groups in favour of those from non-Western cultures. This impacted on everyday clothing as unadulterated forms of traditional dress brought back from the hippy trails of India, the Far East and North Africa, or imported by enterprising retailers, were assimilated into everyday wear.

Thea Porter had been selling kaftans, fabrics, carpets, pillows and other exotic goods from her store, Thea Porter Decorations, in London's Soho since the mid-1960s. She soon started to design and produce the kaftans herself due to overwhelming demand and became a favourite of those in search of the 'authentic' hippy look. Her richly embroidered and distinctive velvet, brocade and silk garments were featured on The Beatles' 'Magical Mystery Tour' album sleeve.

Bill Gibb, Liberty-print dress, 1972. Victoria and Albert Museum, London

Bill Gibb's innovative, fantastical and assured designs drew upon historical and exotic imagery for their inspiration. Medieval dress, Pre-Raphaelite paintings, folk costume of the Near and Far East as well as his native Scotland, traditional North African clothing and the counter-cultural hippy movement found expression within his work. This lavish dress (worn by the pop singer Sandie Shaw) with flowing and full skirt, exaggerated and billowing sleeves, non-Western silhouette and inventive combination of Liberty-print textiles is typical of his work in the early 1970s. Voted *Vogue*'s Designer of the Year in 1970 and having launched his own label in 1972, Gibb developed an international reputation for exemplary workmanship and found favour with celebrities such as Twiggy, Elizabeth Taylor, Bianca Jagger and Anjelica Huston.

Yves Saint Laurent, Evening dress, 1967. The Museum at the Fashion Institute of Technology, New York, US

This dress is from Yves Saint Laurent's 1967 'African' collection and fuses techniques associated with Haute Couture with African motifs and patterns that are intended to evoke traditional tribal clothing and jewellery.

OTHER COLLECTIONS
ENGLAND Fashion Museum, Bath
SCOTLAND Aberdeen Art Gallery and Museum, Aberdeen
US The Costume Institute, Metropolitan Museum of Art, New York

Exoticism; Arts and Crafts; Orientalism; Nostalgic Romanticism

Restorationism; The Birth of Haute Couture; The Internet

Influenced by the refined ready-to-wear vision of Yves Saint Laurent and necessitated by both the need to economise (the sharp rise in oil prices in 1973 affected almost everyone) and the increased number of women in professional employment, there was a revival of timeless classic clothing in which an investment could be made.

GEOFFREY BEENE (1924–2004); JEAN MUIR (1928–95); SONIA RYKIEL (1930–); ROY HALSTON FROWICK (1932–90); YVES SAINT LAURENT (1936–2008); WALTER ALBINI (1941–83); CALVIN KLEIN (1942–)

capsule wardrobe; timeless; practicality; versatility; elegant

Often pilloried as 'the decade that style forgot', the 1970s was the era of pluralistic, anything-goes fashion. Social upheaval and economic instability created a form of sartorial schizophrenia. Styles as disparate as Nostalgic Romanticism, disco, a revival of craft techniques, Glam, sportswear, Punk and Exoticism were underlined by the political activism of the Black is Beautiful and Women's Liberation movements to create a decade that was fast moving, sometimes brash, youthful and vibrant.

Within this maelstrom was a quiet return to good-quality classic styles of elegant, functional and 'no nonsense' clothing. A capsule wardrobe of cigarette-style trousers, knee-length skirts, shirt dresses and simple blouses, jackets and knitwear became timeless staples.

Walter Albini in Milan, Jean Muir in London and Sonia Rykiel in Paris all designed clothing that exhibited elegance and classicism. However, in the spirit of its most important Modernist designer Claire McCardell, New York was at the vanguard of this style and established a reputation for refined, practical and understated clothing that persists to this day.

Calvin Klein, Geoffrey Beene and Roy Halston Frowick all typified the look. Halston opened his own ready-to-wear firm in New York in 1972. The apparently simple lines of the clothing made under the 'Halston Originals' label belied the exemplary technique that produced them. His column dresses, tunic / trouser combinations, shirt dresses and wraparound skirts eschewed unnecessary adornment or gregarious colour, relying instead on butter-soft ultrasuede, cashmere, jersey and silk to provide the drape and sinuosity he was renowned for. While Halston's designs were simple, they were also undeniably sexy and tinged with the glamour of his celebrity friends who included Bianca Jagger, Liza Minelli, Andy Warhol and Steve Rubell of Studio 54.

Providing a more austere form of the Return to Classics was London-based Jean Muir. Self-defined as a designer who rejected fashion in favour of style, Muir worked in a muted palette and was renowned for her deceptively simple, always elegant ensembles. On her 1971 debut in Paris, French *Elle* magazine christened her 'the new queen of the dress'. Muir provided women with a refined, flattering, timeless and easy-to-wear wardrobe that utilised the liquid nature of her favoured fabrics – matte jersey, silks and pliable suede – to great effect. She continued to design in this style until her death in 1991.

Just as Modernism sought to enhance the life of the wearer via its apparent rejection of unnatural restriction, so the Return to Classics continued with its central principle of 'form follows function'. As a fashion it has proved enduring, and the demand for simple, no-nonsense but elegant clothing persists.

→ **Halston beige ultra-suede dress, 1972. The Museum at the Fashion Institute of Technology, New York, US**
The buckskin ultra-suede dress was a signature Halston design and typifies his approach to fashion: luxury, restraint and exemplary technique. His influence can still be seen in the collections of contemporary Minimalists like Calvin Klein, Donna Karan and Narciso Rodriguez.

← **Jean Muir, Ensemble, 1988. National Museum of Costume, Shambellie House, Dumfries and Galloway**
Hailed as the world's greatest dressmaker, Jean Muir excelled at producing timeless designs of technical brilliance. An exemplar of the 'less is more' aesthetic, she eschewed unnecessary adornment, instead relying on high-quality fabrics and exacting cut to produce clothing that was that rarest of things – both critically acclaimed and commercially successful.

OTHER COLLECTIONS
BELGIUM Mode Museum, Antwerp
ENGLAND Fashion Museum, Bath; Victoria and Albert Museum, London
FRANCE Musée de la Mode et du Textile, Louvre, Paris
JAPAN Kyoto Costume Institute, Kyoto
US Los Angeles County Museum of Art, Los Angeles, California; Museum of Art, Rhode Island School of Design, Providence, Rhode Island

Rationalism; Modernism; Minimalism

Rococo; Belle Epoque; Yuppieism

Punk

By the mid-1970s, the heightened aesthetic of Glam and the counter-cultural ethos of the hippy movement had settled into the mainstream. Galvanised by deep discontent with the status quo, the Punk movement emerged in 1975 and expressed its anti-conformist, anti-establishment and disruptive stance through clothing and music.

VIVIENNE WESTWOOD (1941–); MALCOLM McLAREN (1946–); SOO CATWOMAN (SOO LUCAS) (1955–); JORDAN (PAMELA ROOK) (1955–); JOHNNY ROTTEN (JOHN LYDON) (1956–); SID VICIOUS (SIMON RITCHIE) (1957–79); SIOUXSIE SIOUX (SUSAN BALLION) (1957–)

discontent; alienation; disaffection; anti-conformist; Situationist International; subversive; Sex

Vilified and stereotyped by the media, Punks were delineated as kids who were vehemently anti-fashion, anti-establishment and with no more sophisticated a manifesto than to deliberately shock. They could, according to media representations, be identified by a uniform that included dog collars, ripped clothing, part-shaved heads or brightly coloured and spiked hair, safety-pin piercings and tight drainpipe trousers.

These elements all existed, but Punk was in fact an eclectic and highly nuanced culture that drew upon many sources for its evolution and aesthetic. It claimed membership from a diverse range of social backgrounds that can broadly be categorised as disaffected. It had a highly intellectual element inspired by the Situationist International whose critiques of the vacuity of capitalist consumer culture helped to shape the DIY ethos of Punk. Influence can also be traced to sources as varied as Dadaism (the radical French art

↑ Vivienne Westwood and Malcolm McLaren, Sex or Sedionaries bondage trousers and jacket, 1976. Victoria and Albert Museum, London, England
Designed by Westwood and McLaren this outfit borrows elements from traditional suiting, fetish wear, military gear and motorcycle gear. With its crotch-to-bum zipper, terry towelling bum flap and hobble creating bondage straps, it was deeply shocking when first presented but later became the archetypal Punk outfit.

movement of the 1920s that advocated anarchy) which influenced the visual culture as well as the manifesto of Punk, and Andy Warhol's Factory, in particular the nihilistic music of the Velvet Underground and the ripped and safety-pinned clothing of Warhol 'superstar' Jackie Curtis.

However, for an elemental hardcore, Punk was all about the clothes and the look was, quite intentionally, designed to confront. Created through a process of bricolage (the use of disparate materials or styles to create new meaning), Punk style borrowed from the American new-wave music scene, Glam, 1950s rock and roll, fetish wear, reggae and Rastafarian culture and military (including Nazi) memorabilia – it was the way the clothing was put together that created the look. Exemplars of the style included Siouxsie Sioux, Soo Catwoman, Jordan and members of Punk band the Sex Pistols: Johnny Rotten, Paul Cook, Steve Jones and Glen Matlock (later replaced by Sid Vicious).

At the heart of this, and supplying a ready-made version of the Punk look, were Malcolm McLaren (manager of the Sex Pistols) and Vivienne Westwood, proprietors of the clothes shop Sex. Situated at the appropriately named World's End on London's King's Road, the shop name was announced to the passer-by in four-foot-high pink rubber letters and became a provocative purveyor of rubber and bondage fetish wear as well as the appropriately subversive designs of Westwood.

Embodying the aesthetic and the manifesto of the shop (as well as being a source of particular public consternation) were a range of T-shirts emblazoned with provocative imagery and slogans. Designs included two cowboys drawn in profile with their exposed penises almost touching, a print of bare female breasts (called the Tits T-shirt), quotes from Alexander Trocchi's *School for Wives* book of lesbian fantasies, a swastika with the word 'Destroy' printed above and, most controversially, an image of a black leather hood with Cambridge Rapist printed across it.

↓ **Vivienne Westwood and Malcolm McLaren,**
High-heeled shoes, 1974–6, National Gallery
of Victoria, Melbourne, Australia
Fetish wear, which had previously been confined to sex shops and clubs and would have been worn in specialist establishments or in the privacy of one's own home, was brought into the public domain via their shop Sex on London's King's Road by Westwood and McLaren in an act of contrived confrontation.

OTHER COLLECTIONS
ENGLAND Museum of London, London

 Surrealism; New Romanticism; Japanese Avant-Gardeism; Deconstructionism

 Naturalism; Belle Epoque; Nostalgic Romanticism

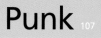

New Romanticism

New Romanticism was an evolution of, rather than a reaction to, the London Punk scene. It emerged in 1978 when the original Punk 'posers' for whom clothing had been the manifesto developed a new look that would distance them from the media-distorted pantomime that Punk had become. Driven by a desire to distinguish themselves from the norm, New Romantics adopted flamboyant, androgynous and highly individual dress.

VIVIENNE WESTWOOD (1941–); DAVID EMANUEL (1952–); ELIZABETH EMANUEL (1953–); ADAM ANT (STUART GODDARD) (1954–); RUSTY EGAN (1957–); STEVE STRANGE (STEVEN HARRINGTON) (1959–); LADY DIANA SPENCER (1961–97); (BOY) GEORGE O'DOWD (1961–)

sartorial extravagance; ingenuity; historical referencing; Glam; androgyny; mainstream adoption

The New Romantic style was pluralistic. If one had the imagination, any look was possible. However, all outfits were united by one shared characteristic: sartorial extravagance. Dressing up and the effort and ingenuity expressed while doing so were what defined this movement. It is usually represented as a swashbuckling and historically referenced style adorned with ribbon, lace and velvet and, although these elements did exist, the influences upon the culture were numerous and the resultant looks diverse. In part it was reminiscent of the visual culture that accompanied Glam: ostentation, androgyny, flamboyance and narcissism being key elements. It was, however, equally as well represented by the futuristic, the Hollywood iconic, the militaristic or the exotic. As long as one had gone to supreme lengths to achieve one's (unique) look, and it showed, one was allowed entry to the club.

New Romanticism flourished in the nightclubs of London. In its earliest incarnation the scene found a home in Billy's in Soho, on a David Bowie themed Tuesday night before moving across town in February 1979 to Blitz. Run by Rusty Egan and Steve Strange (an employee at PX – a clothes shop central to the creation and dissemination of the New Romantic look) with George O' Dowd (Boy George) as cloakroom attendant, the clothing worn and the music played on Tuesday nights at Blitz defined the look and sound of New Romanticism.

This fashion (albeit a palatable and stereotyped version of it) crossed over quite rapidly and without much resistance into the mainstream. It found expression in the unashamedly romantic and flamboyant David and Elizabeth Emmanuel designed wedding dress worn by Lady Diana Spencer for her marriage to Prince Charles in 1981, and was evidenced by the legions of velvet knickerbockers, lace-trimmed high-necked shirts and Adam Ant-style make-up worn at school discos across the UK.

This crossover was initiated by the success of pop stars who were habitues of the underground and London-centric New Romantic scene. Spandau Ballet (Blitz regulars), then Adam Ant and Boy George brought what had been a subversive club look to 'Top of the Pops', a popular music programme that provided a portal to every young person in Britain. Young girls and boys were quick to emulate their new pin-ups and the high street, eager to capitalise on this, provided an affordable and standardised version of the look.

→ **Adam Ant, Theatre costume, 1981. Victoria and Albert Museum, London, England**
The style of Adam Ant, one of the most successful British music acts of the early 1980s, was highly influential within and wholly representative of the New Romantic movement. Influenced by historical, military and tribal dress as well as his contemporaries on the New Romantic scene, he designed all his own stage costumes. This example was worn in the video for the single 'Prince Charming'.

← **Vivienne Westwood and Malcolm McLaren, Woman's 'Pirate' outfit, 1980. Victoria and Albert Museum, London, England**
The 'Pirate' collection utilised historical references and presented the clothing in a theatrical and spectacular way. It was hugely popular and was incorporated into the flourishing New Romantic look.

OTHER COLLECTIONS
JAPAN Kyoto Costume Institute, Kyoto

Revolutionism; Hollywoodism; Glam; Punk; Japanese Avant-Gardeism

Bloomerism; Mass Productionism; The Internet

Football Casualism emerged in the late 1970s, dominated the 1980s and has had a persistent influence upon male working-class fashion to the present day. The look was an amalgamation of pop culture, British heritage style and, in particular, European sports casual labels. The sustained success of British football teams (and most notably Liverpool FC) in European tournaments in the late 1970s until the mid-1980s gave fans an opportunity to visit foreign cities, observe styles and acquire fashion labels not usually available to the British urban working-class male.

ADOLF ('ADI') DASSLER (1900–78); BOBBY MOORE (1941–93); GEORGE BEST (1946–2005); MASSIMO OSTI (1946–2005); BJÖRN BORG (1956–); DAVID BECKHAM (1975–)

sports casual; British heritage; Lois; Fila; Lacoste; adidas; elitism; labels

Fashion has long been a key element of football culture. Players, from testosterone-fuelled Bobby Moore and George Best in the 1960s, through to the metro-sexual and media-friendly David Beckham since the 1990s, have acted as fashion bellwethers for fans and the general public alike. The fashion industry, always keen to capitalise on credibility and mass appeal, has long utilised football stars to promote its goods; and football terraces provided a promenade upon which the British working-class male could exhibit his

sartorial (as well as sporting) allegiances, be that Teddy boy, Mod or Skinhead. However, the late 1970s saw the evolution of a fashion that football could claim as entirely its own: the Casual.

Originating in either Liverpool or Manchester (depending on which accounts are to be believed), Casuals forged a strong sartorial identity and were identifiable by their extreme attention to detail. Favoured garments included jeans by Lois, high-end European sportswear by Ellesse, Fila, Lacoste and Sergio Tachini, outerwear by the Massimo Osti-designed Stone Island and CP Company; footwear by adidas (the creation of Adolf ('Adi') Dassler) and Diadora, and knitwear from Pringle and Lyle & Scott. However, the inherent elitism of the culture meant that there was a remarkable rapidity with which styles and labels came and went out of fashion. Style icons were varied and included the tennis star Björn Borg, golfing legend Arnold Palmer and rock star David Bowie.

Casualism was not a homogeneous culture and, befitting for a fashion tied to the strongly partisan game of football, regional and team-based characteristics were apparent. In a look that mixed soul boy, Punk and pop culture, the earliest Liverpool Casuals favoured a wedge haircut (inspired by David Bowie on the 'Low' album cover), mohair jumpers, plastic sandals and duffle coats; the earliest Manchester Casuals, known as Perry Boys, so-called because of their proclivity for Fred Perry tops, sported a hairstyle known as the 'Failsworth Flick'; and the London-based Casuals, with their pick of the labels, wore Lacoste polo shirts, cashmere scarves, diamond Pringle jumpers and Burberry overcoats – a look heavily influenced by the weekend style of the English gent.

Overly reductive critiques of this subculture assign the tastes of the Casual to random label fetishism or the desire to ape traditionally middle-class codes (hence the dearth of museums with any Football Casual clothing in their archives). However, like all of the dominant working-class subcultures of the post-Second World War period, the Casuals had method in their sartorial choices and a true appreciation of quality and style was evident in their look.

← Sefton Samuels, *Portrait of George Best*, 1968. National Portrait Gallery, London, England
Football casuals are part of very British sartorial heritage. There has always existed a close link between football and a particular form of modern Dandyism, demonstrated by both players and fans alike. George Best was both a football and fashion icon. In this image Best, at 22 years old having been recently named European footballer of the year, is photographed outside his eponymous Manchester fashion boutique in 1968.

← Football Casual ensemble, 1982–4. Victoria and Albert Museum, London, England
This ensemble of Sergio Tacchini tracksuit top, Lacoste polo shirt, Pringle jumper (around waist), Lee jeans and Diadora Björn Borg trainers is typical of the style favoured by Football Casuals in the early 1980s, when hard-to-find European sports labels formed the basis of the look.

 Dandyism; New Edwardianism; New Romanticism

 Bloomerism; Arts and Crafts; Utility

Japanese Avant-Gardeism

TWF

HANAE MORI (1926–); ISSEY MIYAKE (1938–); KENZO TAKADA (1939–); REI KAWAKUBO (1942–); YOHJI YAMAMOTO (1943–)

intellectual; 'beggar look'; subversive; post-Punk; layered

Having debuted in Paris in 1981, the 1982 collections by Rei Kawakubo for Comme des Garçons and Yohji Yamamoto elicited amazement and shock in the fashion world. Both designers featured clothing that defied traditional definition. Models were sent down the catwalk wearing rags in their hair, no make-up and what looked like a bruised bottom lip. The clothes were ragged, bore no relation to the shape of the body and seemed to be obtusely difficult.

In 1984, *GQ* summed up the aesthetic: 'Japanese fashion is different. These are clothes that conform to no fashion standards. They seek to abolish form. They hang loosely on the body in oversized, unusual silhouettes. The colours are almost always monochromatic or black.'

Fashion critics struggled to categorise either the aesthetic or the motivation of the designers. Some, assuming it was a political statement, distastefully referred to it as 'Hiroshima chic' or the 'post Hiroshima look'. Others, struck by the unfinished and ragged nature of the clothing, defined it as the 'beggar' look, 'rag picker chic' or 'bag lady style'. However, the impact upon fashion was unquestionable, with *Liberation* newspaper even declaring: 'French Fashion has found its masters: the Japanese.'

Western assumptions as to what Japanese fashion should be were challenged by the non-cultural specificity of Kawakubo and Yamamoto's collections. Never had Paris entertained subversion to this extent.

Japanese Avante-Garde designers had an explosive impact upon the fashion landscape of the early 1980s. Their intellectual, deconstructed and enveloping designs provided a welcome counterpoint in an era dominated by the aspirational, designer led, vapid, body conscious and power shouldered.

Japanese Avant-Gardeism

For all the frenzy that greeted these collections, they were not without context or precedent. Japanese fashion designers had been a presence in Western fashion from the late 1960s, and Kenzo Takada, Hanae Mori and Issey Miyake were regularly showing collections in Paris from 1977. Miyake, in particular, was a visionary who fused artistic avant-gardeism and adroit technical capabilities with Japanese clothing heritage. In addition both Kawakubo and Yamamoto had long-established fashion businesses based in Tokyo.

Subcultural and subversive fashions also provide a context within which Japanese Avant-Gardeism can be understood. Vivienne Westwood and Malcolm McLaren, with the Punk-associated 'Seditionaries' label, had already explored confrontational Deconstruction in their collections. Indeed,

the term post-Punk has been used to describe the Japanese Avant-Garde look. Also, the fashion that became New Romantic showed parallels with the layered, enveloping Japanese silhouette (if not the details or agenda) and was contemporaneously being explored in London clubs and on the catwalk by Westwood.

All these designers are now part of the fashion establishment where their influence has been pervasive.

← **Rei Kawakubo for Comme des Garçons, Ensemble, 1982. Victoria and Albert Museum, London, England**
Rei Kawakubo has continued to challenge normative Western definitions of what constitutes beauty. Purposely 'deforming' the jumper with what appears to be randomly placed holes defies the commonly accepted endeavours of fashion to enhance, flatter and present perfection.

← **Yohji Yamamoto, Jacket dress and pants, 1983. Kyoto Costume Institute, Kyoto, Japan**
The colourless, deliberately torn and enveloping fashions presented by Yamamoto and Kawakubo in Paris in 1982 shocked the fashion world and raised questions about Western definitions of beauty. Although hailed as a revolution by some, on the whole this display of 'conscious destitution' was met with a mixture of amusement, bemusement and confusion, and was categorised in suitably reductive terms as the 'beggar' or 'ragged' look.

OTHER COLLECTIONS
AUSTRALIA Powerhouse Museum, Sydney
BELGIUM Mode Museum, Antwerp
FRANCE Musée de la Mode et du Textile, Louvre, Paris
JAPAN Kobe Fashion Museum, Kobe, Japan
NORTHERN IRELAND Ulster Museum, Belfast
SPAIN Museo del Traje, Madrid
US The Costume Institute, Metropolitan Museum of Art, New York

 Punk; New Romanticism; Deconstructionism

 Empire Revivalism; Hollywoodism; Nostalgic Romanticism

Yuppieism

The 1980s came to be defined by the most acquisitive, status-driven, conservative and designer-focused style tribe of the 20th century: the Yuppies. Originally a term coined by advertisers to categorise a new breed of consumer in the 1980s, the designer-clad, wide-shouldered, power-suited 'Yuppie' (an acronym for young upwardly mobile professional person) has come to symbolise the unashamed materialism and self-obsession of the decade.

RONALD REAGAN (1911–2004); MARGARET THATCHER (1925–); **GIORGIO ARMANI** (1934–); **RALPH LAUREN** (1939–); **CALVIN KLEIN** (1942–); **THIERRY MUGLER** (1948–)

acquisitive; status symbol; designer; shoulder pads; power suit; materialism; *Dress for Success*

Affluent and conspicuously status conscious, image was everything to the Yuppie. The stereotypical Yuppie aspired to live in sleek black, grey and white minimal interiors filled with designer goods and high-tech gadgets; they drove cars that were fast, sporty and bought to impress; and post work they would not go to the pub, but instead to a wine bar, representative of their continental affiliations and rejection of traditional make-do values.

Reflecting their go-getting and uncompromising values, the style adopted by the Yuppie was (the appropriately named) power dressing. For men this was an exaggerated form of the classic male business suit: lapels were deeper, shoulders wider and jackets double breasted, a silhouette reminiscent of classic 1930s tailoring. Women, influenced by the writings of John Molloy in *Dress for Success* (a guide to appropriate dress for women

in the work place) and hoping to ape the career paths of their male colleagues, also adopted the power suit.

The power suit took sartorial cues from the male executive. Silhouettes were linear and boxy so as not to emphasise the feminine; jackets were double breasted with wide lapels; skirts were knee length and straight; colours were chosen from either a restrained palette of navy and beige or were bold and assertive in shades of red or royal blue; and wide, padded shoulders that gave a triangular silhouette were essential, and indeed have become shorthand for 1980s Yuppie fashions.

The rise of the Yuppie was a consequence of very particular sociopolitical circumstances. The election of the Conservative Margaret Thatcher in the UK and her ideological counterpart in the US, Ronald Reagan, coincided with an era of sustained economic prosperity. This was

→ **Giorgio Armani, Pant suits, 1985–9.**
Kyoto Costume Institute, Kyoto, Japan
Analogous to the rise of the Yuppie was the development of a new breed of fashion super-company: the designer brand. Calvin Klein, Ralph Lauren and their ilk operated like highly evolved marketing machines peddling entire lifestyles to the conspicuous consumers of the 1980s. Labels became status symbols and wearing them was a shorthand way of denoting that you had made it, an important aspiration in the era of the Yuppie. Giorgio Armani, the Milan-based designer, was at the vanguard of this development in fashion, and his strong-shouldered, loosely tailored suits were adopted by men and women keen to display their self-assurance. Armani, an astute businessman, was quick to capitalise on his popularity and talismanic status and launched a plethora of products and ranges bearing his name.

encouraged by policies of favourable taxation for private enterprise and cuts in state subsidies. According to Thatcher we were individuals and as such had to take responsibility for our own welfare. Anything we wanted was within our grasp if only we worked hard enough. Yuppie fashion was wholly representative of this new conservatism.

However, this trend was not limited to the boardroom and one did not need the qualifications, the job or the earnings to dress like a Wall Street executive. High-street companies, usually focused on providing youthful disposable fashions in opposition to the establishment, peddled the 1980s Yuppie existence in their ranges and advertising campaigns.

← Thierry Mugler, Ensemble, early 1980s.
The Costume Institute, Metropolitan Museum of Art, New York, US
The French fashion designer Thierry Mugler pioneered the big-shouldered power look that became a hallmark of 1980s fashion. His angular, bold and powerful clothes presented a futuristic and angular definition of exaggerated femininity that filtered into the mainstream.

OTHER COLLECTIONS
AUSTRALIA National Gallery of Victoria, Melbourne; Powerhouse Museum, Sydney
ENGLAND Gallery of Costume, Platt Hall, Manchester; Victoria and Albert Museum, London
US Arizona Costume Institute, Phoenix Art Museum, Phoenix, Arizona; Los Angeles Country Museum of Art, Los Angeles, California

 Savile Row; Utility; Return to Classics

 Revolutionism; Neoclassicism; Deconstructionism

Grunge

↓ V-neck sweater formerly owned by Kurt Cobain, c 1992. Experience Music Project, Science Fiction Museum and Hall of Fame, Seattle, Washington, US
Kurt Cobain was the reluctant poster boy for the Grunge movement and his clothing style was aped by both fans of his music and those who simply wished to emulate his dishevelled, counter-cultural style. He wore this green v-neck sweater on the cover of the January 1992 issue of US music magazine *Spin*.

Grunge fashion had its origins in the Seattle-based music scene of the same name. Characterised by its lack of polish or artifice as well as its affordability, Grunge can be read as a reaction to the yuppiedom and moneyed excess of the 1980s. However, what began as the clothing of a counterculture rapidly spread to the mainstream and became the first major fashion development unique to the 1990s.

MARC JACOBS (1964–); COURTNEY LOVE (1964–); STEVEN MEISEL (1954–); ANNA SUI (1964–); KURT COBAIN (1967–94); CHRISTIAN FRANCIS ROTH (1969–)

Nirvana; *Sassy* magazine; Generation X; commercialisation; appropriation

Grunge rapidly evolved from subculture to mainstream fashion in 1992. It was mainly MTV's heavy promotion of Grunge bands, in particular Nirvana, that accelerated the dissemination of the look. In the US, *Sassy* magazine was closely associated with the promotion of Grunge and thrift styles for teenage girls. Hollywood provided its own take with the release of 'Grunge' movie *Singles* (1992). All of this was compounded by the media packaging and preoccupation with the supposedly disaffected youth of Generation X.

A stereotypical Grunge outfit consisted of layers of dishevelled and mismatched clothing. Men and women sported lank, long hair and wore plaid shirts, torn and cut-off jeans over thermal long johns with combat boots or Converse All Stars (canvas and rubber basketball shoes). Incongruity was also a feature, particularly for women, as pretty floral tea dresses and vintage silk slips were worn with heavy boots and oversized cardigans. Nirvana frontman Kurt

Cobain and his wife Courtney Love became the poster boy and girl for Grunge.

Predictably, if remarkably quickly, Grunge was commercialised and what had been an alternative to mainstream fashion was appropriated by the establishment. In 1992 designers Anna Sui, Christian Francis Roth and Xuly Bet created Grunge-inspired collections and in December the same year American *Vogue*, the bastion of conservative fashion, produced a 10-page Grunge spread. With photographs by Steven Meisel and the title 'Grunge and Glory', *Vogue* here explained to its readers that Grunge 'had broken out of the clubs, garages and thrift shops of Seattle to dominate rock radio, MTV and the aspirations of kids across America'.

Most notorious, though, was Marc Jacobs, creative director at US fashion house Perry Ellis, who controversially took thrift-store staples and re-imagined them in luxury fabrics. His presentation of cashmere long johns, 'flannel' shirts made of washed silk, heavy army-style boots and crocheted skull caps worn over lank and unwashed hair was rapturously received by the fashion press and prompted *Women's Wear Daily* to describe him as 'the guru of grunge'. But commercially it was a disaster. The huge price tags attached to thrift-style clothing angered consumers, sales were dismal and Jacobs lost his job.

However, the commercial failure and the short-lived nature of the fashion belies the far-reaching impact of Grunge on the aesthetic of the 1990s. From 1993 a more palatable take on the trend was adopted by established designers such as Calvin Klein, who used the Grungy and markedly waif-like model Kate Moss in his advertisements.

← **Ensemble, date unknown. Victoria and Albert Museum, London, England**
Typically comprised of thrift-store clothing layered to create a dishevelled style, Grunge provided a counterpoint to the excess of the 1980s. This ensemble of worn jeans, plaid shirt, leather paratrooper boots, striped sweater and cotton T-shirt is typical of the look.

OTHER COLLECTIONS
ENGLAND Brighton Museum and Art Gallery, Brighton
US Rock and Roll Hall of Fame and Museum, Cleveland, Ohio

 Revolutionism; Punk; New Romanticism; Deconstructionism

 Restorationism; Belle Epoque; Yuppieism; Celebrity Consumerism

Deconstructionism

Widely influential during the 1990s and closely associated with Belgian fashion design, Deconstructionism subverted traditional notions of garment construction and endeavoured to re-evaluate the meaning of clothes and how they are worn.

MARTIN MARGIELA (1957–); WALTER VAN BIERENDONCK (1957–); DRIES VAN NOTEN (1958–); DIRK BIKKEMBERGS (1959–); ANN DEMEULEMEESTER (1959–); RICK OWENS (1962–); VIKTOR HORSTING (1969–); ROLF SNOEREN (1969–)

Belgian fashion; construction; meaning; conceptual; refashioning; Surrealist

Often characterised as the literal 'taking apart' and reconstruction of clothing to reveal seams, frayed hems and the inner workings of garments, Deconstructionism (following in the tradition of Punk and Japanese Avant-gardeism) can more broadly be understood as challenging conventional attitudes towards the design, presentation and consumption of clothing.

Emerging in the late 1980s and exerting a palpable influence upon the aesthetic of the 1990s, Deconstructionism has become closely associated with Belgian fashion design and in particular the work of Martin Margiela. A graduate of the Royal Academy of Fine Arts in Antwerp, Margiela was part of a wave of designers (including Anne Demeulemeester, Dries van Noten, Walter van Bierendonck and Dirk Bikkembergs) who launched their own collections in the late 1980s and established Belgium as a credible fashion source.

Having worked with Jean Paul Gaultier as an assistant designer from 1984, Margiela launched his eponymous label in spring/summer 1998 to huge critical acclaim. A recurring theme has been reclamation and recycling, whereby existing objects (fashion and otherwise) are refashioned to create a new garment. Leather gloves have become a halter-neck top; ballet shoes an evening bag; army-issue socks a jumper; broken plates a waistcoat; and old incongruous garments are pulled apart and fused with others to create a new whole. Some collections have explored the Surrealist device of trompe l'oeil while others have played with proportion and dimension.

Described as the JD Salinger of the fashion world and the purveyor of a 'cult of impersonality', Margiela is a famously 'anonymous' designer who refuses to claim authorship for the design of the clothes, referring instead to Maison Martin Margiela, the collective, and attaching a plain white label to garments with no obvious clues as to their provenance.

However, although Margiela's designs have invited intellectual examination, been presented as installations in art galleries, inspired fetishistic reverence among the fashion cognoscenti and consistently questioned and subverted traditional fashion practices, Maison Martin Margiela is a commercially successful company that operates wholly within the parameters of the fashion system. Owned by Renzo Russo (founder of Diesel), the company has a multitude of stores worldwide, is regularly featured in magazines, presents fashion collections twice a year and has licensed the production of its collections to various companies.

As a clothing tradition, the principles of Deconstructionism have continued to influence fashion designers of the late 20th and 21st centuries. Of particular note are Viktor and Rolf (Viktor Horsting and Rolf Snoering), Rick Owens and Jun Takahashi of Undercover.

← **Martin Margiela, Jacket, 1997.**
Kyoto Costume Institute, Kyoto, Japan
This jacket is a replica of a dress form by Stockman, the pioneer of standardised dummies for use in the manufacture of clothing at the end of the 19th century, and presents a multilayered comment on fashion and fashion objects . It reveals Margiela's love of and fascination with the craft of the dressmaker. It utilises the Surrealist device of displacement – the placing of an object or image in an unfamiliar and jarring location – to draw attention to, and change the meaning of, the original, and raises questions about the female body and the standardised ideals peddled by the fashion industry.

↙ **Ann Demeulemeester, Trouser suit, 1993.**
Powerhouse Museum, Sydney, Australia
Ann Demeulemeester is a graduate of the Royal Academy of Fine Arts in Antwerp and is one of the 'Antwerp Six', a group that helped to establish Belgian fashion on the world stage when they presented their collections at London Fashion Week in 1988 to huge critical acclaim. Her philosophy of 'design and not decoration' is embodied in this suit: the lean, androgynous and unstructured silhouette, deliberate creases, muted colour and subtly deconstructed tailoring techniques are typical of her designs, which continually reference and rework a similar aesthetic.

OTHER COLLECTIONS
AUSTRALIA National Gallery of Victoria, Melbourne
BELGIUM Modemuseum, Hasselt; Mode Museum, Antwerp
ENGLAND Victoria and Albert Museum, London
THE NETHERLANDS Centraal Museum, Utrecht
NORTHERN IRELAND Ulster Museum, Belfast
SWEDEN Moderna Museet, Stockholm
US The Costume Institute, Metropolitan Museum of Art, New York; Los Angeles County Museum of Art, Los Angeles, California

 Surrealism; Japanese Avant-Gardeism; Punk; Grunge

Neoclassicism; Yuppieism; Celebrity Consumerism

Postmodernism

 Whereas Modernism was characterised by logic, simplicity, a break from history and functionality, the Postmodern age dispensed with linearity in favour of eclecticism, parody and cultural hybridity.

KARL LAGERFELD (1938–); **FRANCO MOSCHINO** (1950–94)

pluralism; pastiche; parody; cultural hybridity; fragmentation; bricolage

Postmodernism is a loosely defined concept that literally means 'after Modernism'. Theoretically, this denotes the rejection of grand narratives, social hierarchies, the distinction between low and high culture and autocratic institutions. Instead, the Postmodern age was one of pluralism and fragmentation. Fashion, particularly from the 1960s, clearly expressed these characteristics.

Fashion in the Postmodern age has become fast moving, heterogeneous, culturally non-specific, democratic and intertextual. No longer can we talk of one fashion, but instead have the choice of many. A guide to the modes for spring/summer 2009, published by the UK *Vogue*, delineated a multitude of key trends for the season. Trousers could be slim and tailored, pyjama-style, skinny or voluminous; fashionable textiles were varied and included the metallic, the sheer, the optical and the African inspired; and colours ranged from barely there nudes to electrifying and vivid hues. Anything, it would seem, goes.

The sheer proliferation of styles available to the Postmodern fashion consumer demonstrates the breaking down of old hierarchies, whereby fashion was autocratic and 'trickled down' to the masses from above. Fashion inspiration is now multifarious. A look can just as easily be inspired by street style, subcultures, musical genre, a historical era or, with the rapidity of contemporary globalisation, from cultures other than one's own.

Bricolage, the practice of adopting and recombining diverse and existing styles into a new whole, has become a leitmotif of individuals and designers in the Postmodern age. This appropriation of incongruous elements within an outfit and the use of cultural symbols without reference to their original purpose debases their meaning, creating new and (post-modern) connotations. Related to, but distinct from, bricolage is the relentless and continual plundering of the past. This can either take the form of pastiche (an imitation of a style) or parody (a satirical copy). Critics level that the random cannibalisation of past fashions has spawned a culture in which creativity is exhausted and the new no longer exists, though this criticsim could equally be levelled at Worth's crinolines or Dior's 'New Look'.

Other Postmodern characteristics can be explained by tangible developments within the fashion industry. The proliferation of publications dedicated to fashion and its consumption; the technological advances made in quick-response production techniques; the resultant strength of high-street fashion; the rise of magazines devoted to subcultures; and the impact of the Internet have all produced a fashion system within which rapid dissemination, appropriation, plurality, cultural hybridity and nostalgia dominate.

← **John Galliano for Christian Dior, Dress and jacket, 2000. Arizona Costume Institute, Phoenix Art Museum, Phoenix, Arizona, US**
John Galliano's designs, for both his eponymous label and as chief designer at Christian Dior, draw upon an eclectic range of sources for inspiration. Practising a form of bricolage he can, within a single collection, juxtapose seemingly incongruous elements to present a singularly Postmodern vision that fuses high and low culture, combines multitudinous historical references and recontextualises indigenous and traditional costume within high fashion. The silhouette of this chiffon bias-cut dress is reminiscent of the gowns popular in 1930s Hollywood. The fabric is printed to appear as if made from worn denim and makes reference to the rugged chic of the Wild West, and the jacket, with its bold, metal features mimics the contemporary use of heavy fastenings within the rap music scene.

↓ **Karl Lagerfeld for Chanel, Ensemble, 1991. Fashion Museum, Bath, England**
Karl Lagerfeld, the chief designer at the House of Chanel since 1983, is an arch Postmodernist who regularly fuses high and low culture within his collections. In this outfit he has presented a mischievous Postmodern reworking of the classic Chanel two-piece tweed suit. The jacket, a garment that has become a symbol of bourgeois respectability, is made from wool blended with pink lurex, and the skirt is made from the most utilitarian of fabrics, denim. While some might decry his use of (relatively) cheap and everyday fabrics within the Chanel collections as sacrilege, Lagerfeld is simply continuing a tradition started by Coco Chanel herself: the appropriation of everyday and sporting items into high fashion.

OTHER COLLECTIONS
AUSTRIA Wien Museum, Vienna
ENGLAND Brighton Museum and Art Gallery, Brighton; Victoria and Albert Museum, London
ITALY Galleria del Costume, Palazzo Pitti, Florence
SWEDEN Nordic Museum, Stockholm
US Museum of Art, Rhode Island School of Design, Providence, Rhode Island

◉ Surrealism; Vintage

◒ Modernism; Space Ageism; Japanese Avant-Gardeism

Minimalism

 Closely related to Modernism, Minimalism refers to a refined and reductive aesthetic that lacks temporality. It has been a recurring theme in the fashions of the 20th and 21st centuries. Following in the tradition of Coco Chanel, Claire McCardell and Jean Muir, a number of designers working with a pared-down aesthetic came to prominence in the 1990s.

CALVIN KLEIN (1942–); JIL SANDER (1943–); SHIRIN GUILD (1946–); HELMUT LANG (1956–)

reductive; restrained; intellectual; functional; 'less is more'

The 1980s were characterised (and caricatured) as a brash era of big shoulders, designer labels and an absence of good taste. Almost as though the change in decade demanded that this excess be redressed, the 1990s exhibited a more restrained and intellectual aesthetic that eschewed the 'look at me' of the previous decade. Alongside the dishevelment of Grunge and the austere intellectualism of Deconstructionism there developed a trend for Minimalist clothing.

Following in the tradition of Modernism, Minimalism was a restrained, functional aesthetic. However, Minimalists displayed a rigour and intellectualism that set them apart from designers who simply follow a classic line in their clothing. The refined and elegant tailoring of masculine clothing was incorporated into a feminine aesthetic; colours were neutral or subdued so as not to distract from the cut (or the wearer); and unnecessary embellishments were dispensed with.

Jil Sander is closely associated with the Minimalist style and her designs of the 1990s exemplify the great skill required to produce beautiful clothing that requires no

embellishment for its interest. Having already established her business in Germany, Sander's 1993 debut in Paris was a directional and assured presentation that favoured simple lines and displayed architectural considerations. Sander left her own label under a cloud in 2000, and attempts to retain the original Minimalist allure of the brand fell short. However, since 2005, under the guidance of Belgian designer Raf Simons, Jil Sander clothing has again become worthy of its earlier reputation.

The Austrian designer Helmut Lang, although his work crossed over into an exploration of Deconstruction, was an arch Minimalist who described his clothing as 'non-referential'. Defined by a lean silhouette, juxtaposition of incongruous and sometimes obviously synthetic materials (such as reflective tape) and androgynous collections, Lang's designs were the embodiment of 1990s Minimalism.

Shirin Guild, Linen ensemble, 1996.
Victoria and Albert Museum, London, England
Shirin Guild occupies a unique position within the trend for Minimalism since the 1990s; she incorporates elements of traditional menswear from her native Iran into a very particular aesthetic. This outfit, which envelops the body and is composed of square and T-shaped garments, has been fashioned from the finest linen in muted shades of grey. The trousers, with their apron-like over-skirt, mimic the use of layered clothing worn by Iranian peasants who seek warmth in an inclement climate.

Calvin Klein, 'Bernadette' day dress, 1996.
Victoria and Albert Museum, London, England
Oft referred to as the master of Minimalism, Calvin Klein has, since the 1990s, perfected the 'less is more' approach to fashion. The focus of this dress is on cut and fabric, and the simple lines, elegant silhouette and lack of adornment typify the Minimalist aesthetic.

OTHER COLLECTIONS
AUSTRALIA Powerhouse Museum, Sydney
AUSTRIA Modesammlung des Historischen Museums, Vienna
BELGIUM Mode Museum, Antwerp
CANADA Costume Museum of Canada, Winnipeg
NORTHERN IRELAND Ulster Museum, Belfast
US The Museum at the Fashion Institute of Technology, New York

Rationalism; Modernism; Deconstructionism

Belle Epoque; New Edwardianism; Rococo

4

21ST CENTURY

Introduction

Fashion in the 21st century is an extremely fast-moving, heterogeneous system in which more people than ever before are able to participate. This has been facilitated by the further dissolution of social hierarchies, the communication revolution that accompanied the widespread adoption of the Internet, the breaking down of international trade barriers and the technological refinement of advanced and responsive production methods.

Internet; globalisation; high-street fashion; pluralism

Historically – and particularly in the 1960s – representations of the 21st century in film, literature and the media portrayed a technologically advanced society in which humans lived alongside robots, food was substituted with pills and clothes would no longer follow fashion cycles but instead would be shaped by scientific progress. The reality has proved to be somewhat more mundane and fashion in the first decade of the century has been an evolution of all that was initiated towards the end of the previous century.

The widespread adoption of the Internet by both industry and consumer has arguably had the greatest impact upon the way that fashion has evolved in the 21st century. It is the first tool that has allowed truly democratic participation in the business and culture of fashion. Now anyone can start their own fashion blog, join a discussion forum, produce their own online magazine or set up a business selling their own designs.

The clearest expression of the rapidity with which fashion now moves is to be found on the British high street, which in the past 10 years has undergone something of a renaissance. Having experienced an extended period as the poor relation of the fashion industry, lagging with trends and used only if one could not afford to go elsewhere, the high street is now an integral, directional and much respected sector of the fashion market providing super-fast and super-affordable clothing to a highly fashion-conscious market. This transformation has been facilitated by technological innovation, the breaking down of old fashion hierarchies, the rise of publications dedicated to this sector of the market, and clever marketing on the part of the high-street companies themselves. Topshop has been at the vanguard of the resurrection.

However the rapidity, affordability and widespread dissemination of all fashions has become something of a double-edged sword. Fashion is now so pluralistic and fast moving that it has been accused of becoming tired and increasingly normalised; that it is no longer possible to be radical in fashion because we live in an era where anything goes.

Whereas the second half of the 20th century was characterised by the increasing conspicuousness of sub-cultural and counter-cultural fashions that challenged the status quo and aroused moral alarm and public debate, this century has so far been bereft of any truly outsider fashions. The speed at which any sub-cultural movement is now identified and plundered by a rapacious fashion industry neuters its impact and increases the rate at which fashion moves on.

Rebecca Earley, Ensemble made from recycled materials, 2006. The Crafts Council Collection, London, England
The inherent wastefulness, poor use of resources and over-consumption promoted by the fashion industry has aroused criticism from both those within and outside it. Designers and manufacturers have begun to make some attempts to address this and the 21st century has seen a significant increase in the number of eco-fashion companies. This jacket is made from recycled materials and was originally exhibited as part of a project entitled 'Well Fashioned: Eco Style in the UK'. The aim of this was to explore the idea that fashion could be stylish, well conceived and eco-conscious as well as considering how eco-fashion could evolve and become an integral part of the fashion industry.

↓ **Louis Vuitton, 'Speedy' travelling bag, 2001. Powerhouse Museum, Sydney, Australia**
This classic Louis Vuitton monogrammed travelling bag has apparently been defaced with silver-painted graffiti and is the result of a collaboration between New York artist Stephen Sprouse and Vuitton's chief designer Marc Jacobs. An explosion in the popularity of designer handbags has meant that this has become an extremely lucrative market for fashion houses and virtually all of them have produced designs to satisfy consumer demand for what is known as the 'it bag'. This phenomenon has been catalysed by clever marketing schemes that capitalise on the power of celebrity endorsement whereby a bag photographed on the arm of the right person guarantees its success. The 'Speedy' became the 'it-bag' of 2001 and sales were reputed to have been in excess of $300 million.

KEY COLLECTIONS
BELGIUM Mode Museum, Antwerp
ENGLAND Victoria and Albert Museum, London
JAPAN Kyoto Costume Institute, Kyoto
US Los Angeles County Museum of Art, Los Angeles, California; The Costume Institute, Metropolitan Museum of Art, New York

The Internet has revolutionised the business and culture of fashion. The way that fashion is shopped for, communicated and discussed has become a more democratic process whereby one's location, age, mobility or fashion experience does not preclude participation.

NATALIE MASSENET (1965–); NICK ROBERTSON (1968–); SCOTT SCHUMAN (1968–); SUSIE BUBBLE (SUSANNA LAU) (1984–)

technological progress; accessibility; e-commerce; innovation; democratisation; fashion blog

Technological progress is the catalyst that has transformed fashion from being the preserve of the idle rich to an accessible pleasure for everyone. The Industrial Revolution, which was bound up with advances in textile production, eventually precipitated the mass manufacture of clothing. Improvements in the speed and quality and lowered production costs of the printing press impacted directly upon the dissemination and rapidity of fashion; the development of synthetic materials in the early 20th century made fashion a more affordable and practical prospect for the masses; and the evolution of film, television and music media has had a direct influence on the clothing worn by the average consumer. However, it can reasonably be argued that it has been since the development of the Internet that we have witnessed the most seismic of shifts in the business and culture of fashion.

Established fashion retailers were initially suspicious of and resistant to the merits of online retail. Working on the (rational) assumption that shopping for clothes is a sensual experience and that things have to be touched, tried on and seen in their three-dimensional glory before a purchase is made, inhibited the early development of fashion e-commerce. But this has become one of the strongest and fastest growing sectors of both the Internet and fashion economies. In 2009 Neilsen Online (an Internet market research company) reported that in the last quarter of 2008 the home and fashion sector of the Internet market had experienced growth five times that of any comparable category. Also, as the high street buckles under the increasing costs of traditional retail, fashion e-commerce is bucking all trends and reports a healthy growth.

This success can be attributed to innovative marketing, a pleasurable customer experience, accessibility and the democratic nature of shopping on the Internet. There is no pressure or judgement from sales assistants, so the process can be relatively anonymous. Delivery can be ultra-fast, clothing can be tried on in the comfort of one's home and returned (often at no extra cost) if not appropriate, the choice is immense, pricing is competitive, advances in picture quality and zoom facilities allow close inspection of garments, and the innovative layout of websites provides consumers with a visual feast akin to that of reading a favourite magazine. So powerful is the Internet in the fashion economy that the fastest growing fashion retailer in the UK is a company with absolutely no high-street presence and which exists only online: ASOS.com.

The Internet has also democratised consumer participation in the culture of fashion. No longer is fashion communicated by an elite to a passive audience via the printed or televised media. The fashion blog, a means by which anybody can set up their own website and communicate their

NET-A-PORTER.COM

| WHAT'S NEW | DESIGNERS | BOUTIQUES | CLOTHING | LINGERIE | BAGS | SHOES | ACCESSORIES | MAGAZINE | VIDEO |

BANDAGE DRESSING
25 ways to wrap up your look
Watch it! Shop it!

LEGWORK
Make leggings your spring foundation

BLUE BELLE
Shop the cool cobalt hits you need now

FOR net-a-porter
THE EXCLUSIVE COLLABORATION IS HERE...

sartorial preferences, discoveries and observations, has given a voice to those previously marginalised from traditional forms of fashion media. The more popular of these sites, such as Style Bubble (created by Susie Bubble), Garance Dore, Facehunter and Scott Schuman's Sartorialist, have huge dedicated followings and are now revered within the fashion industry as offering a fresh and up-to-date perspective on contemporary fashion.

Net-a-porter.com online fashion retail
Founded in 2000 by Natalie Massenet, net-a-porter.com has been at the vanguard of the online retail of high fashion. Hugely successful and hailed by British *Vogue* as 'revolutionising the way we buy designer clothes', net-a-porter.com defied the commonly held wisdom that shopping for expensive and exclusive clothing on the Internet would be untenable, and continues to innovate and lead the market in this field.

OTHER COLLECTIONS
CELEBRITY AND MODEL FASHION
gofugyourself.celebuzz.com; thecoolhunter.net
E-COMMERCE SITES asos.com; net-a-porter.com; topshop.com
FASHION AND ART showstudio.com
FORUMS purseforum.com
ONLINE MAGAZINES style.com
PERSONAL BLOGS kingdomofstyle.typepad.co.uk; stylebubble.typepad.com
STREET FASHION facehunter.blogspot.com; garancedore.fr; thesartorialist.blogspot.com

 Industrialism; Mass Productionism; Celebrity Consumerism

 Revolutionism; Arts and Crafts; Football Casualism

Celebrity Consumerism

◖ Celebrities are the sartorial bellwethers of the Postmodern age. Traditional hierarchies whereby the masses sought to emulate the fashions created and worn by the upper classes have broken down and instead our aspirations are fixed on the figure of the celebrity.

◖ **CATHY McGOWAN** (1943–); **GIANNI VERSACE** (1946–97); **ELIZABETH HURLEY** (1965–); **SARAH JESSICA PARKER** (1965–); **ASHLEY OLSEN** (1986–); **MARY-KATE OLSEN** (1986–)

◖ Postmodern; emulation; aspiration; age of celebrity; coolspotters; endorsement

◖ We are, it is said, living in an age of celebrity, in which there is a heightened fascination with and unquenchable appetite for information on where they go, what they do and who they do it with. Analogous to this has been the effect of the celebrity upon our consumption patterns, most obviously expressed in the contemporary obsession with celebrity fashion.

A commercial framework has been constructed to capitalise on this fascination with the style of the celebrity. On the Internet, sites like As Seen On Screen (asos.com) specialise in selling replica and original versions of clothing worn by celebrities, and coolspotters (coolspotters.com), although not a direct retail site, provides a one-stop portal to identifying the products, brands and fashions worn by particular celebrities and their fictional alter egos. Magazines wholly devoted to celebrity fashion provide commentary on their style and offer step-by-step guides to getting the look, and the letters pages are filled with requests as to where one can go to purchase celebrity-endorsed items. Designers, aware of the influence of celebrity upon their own profiles, strategically ally themselves with those who are representative of the image they wish to project.

Celebrities have not restricted their endorsement of products to associating with, starring in the advertisements for or wearing the clothing of a particular designer, and (not letting a lack of fashion training get in the way of a good money spinner) many famous faces have now put their weight behind their own-name celebrity brands. Some are known for their sense of style and use their sartorial credibility to carry them through; ranges like Sarah Jessica Parker's 'Bitten' for US budget retailer Steve and Barry's and 'The Row' by Olsen twins Ashley and Mary-Kate do not stretch the credulity of the consumer. Others, although perhaps well dressed, have no more than a spurious association with fashion: 'Sweetface' by Jennifer Lopez and 'Mblem' by Mandy Moore being a case in point.

Although we are experiencing a heightened version of Celebrity Consumerism, this phenomenon is not, however, exclusive to the 21st century. Hollywood and its stars in the 1930s exerted a huge influence upon contemporary fashions. The studios thus promoted copies of popular outfits and magazines dedicated to replicating the styles onscreen became popular. In the 1960s the outfits worn by Cathy McGowan, presenter of British music show 'Ready Steady Go!', were copied slavishly by young women encouraging McGowan to launch a celebrity-endorsed clothing range.

Gianni Versace, Evening dresses, 1996 and Spring/Summer 1991. The Costume Institute, Metropolitan Museum of Art, New York, US
It could reasonably be argued that Gianni Versace, having recognised the glamour, excitement and commercial pull that surrounded them, was a key catalyst in the contemporary veneration of celebrities within the fashion industry. He filled the front row of his shows with celebrity faces, and on the catwalk always used celebrity supermodels. His overtly sexy outfits have been worn by and made the careers of numerous celebrities (most notably Elizabeth Hurley who wore a headline-grabbing safety-pinned Versace dress to the premiere of her boyfriend Hugh Grant's movie), and the adverts have featured the faces of celebrity icons including Madonna, Courtney Love, Halle Berry and Britney Spears. The example on the right was designed for US singing superstar Tina Turner.

OTHER COLLECTIONS
AUSTRALIA Powerhouse Museum, Sydney
ENGLAND Fashion Museum, Bath; Gallery of Costume, Platt Hall, Manchester; Victoria and Albert Museum, London
ITALY Galleria del Costume, Palazzo Pitti, Florence
US Chicago History Museum, Chicago, Illinois

 Hollywoodism; Postmodernism; Brand Revivalism

 Bloomerism; Utility; Japanese Avant-Gardeism

Brand Revivalism

 A symptom of the huge costs involved in establishing a new designer's name as well as being typical of our retrogressive and piecemeal Postmodern age, the revival of defunct or underperforming fashion brands has accelerated to an unprecedented degree in the last decade. What began in earnest with the appointment of Tom Ford at Gucci in 1994 has picked up huge momentum since the turn of the millennium.

ALBER ELBAZ (1961–); **TOM FORD** (1961–); **BELLA FREUD** (1961–); **NICOLAS GHESQUIÈRE** (1971–); **PHILIP LIM** (1973–); **OLIVIER THEYSKENS** (1977–); **CHRISTOPHER KANE** (1982–)

heritage; marketing; pedigree; gravitas; nostalgia

The revival of formerly successful and prestigious fashion brands has become a pronounced trend in the last decade. The reasons for this are easily understood. Why start a new business when you can build on the heritage of an established if defunct brand? The hugely powerful and market-savvy conglomerates that now control a huge stake in the fashion industry have realised this and have gone about purchasing and relaunching such labels. In a highly competitive market where the vast majority of new businesses fail within their first 18 months, this is a canny mechanism that helps to reduce risk and provides a short cut to the good will, heritage and cultural capital of an established name with a fine pedigree. The need for excessive introductory advertising is circumvented and gravitas is immediate.

This technique has been employed with varying degrees of success. Those that carry it off tend to be respectful of, but are not defined by, a company's

heritage. Innovation and relevance are key. Those who have prevailed include Alber Elbaz who was appointed head designer at Lanvin in 2001, transforming it from a staid Paris institution into one of the most revered fashion houses of the 21st century. The appointment of the Modernist Nicolas Ghesquière as creative director at Balenciaga has revived the fortunes of what was once the most influential couture house in Paris, and the resurrection of first Rochas in 2005 and then Nina Ricci in 2007 was carried out successfully under the auspices of young Belgian designer Olivier Theyskens.

However, for every success there are numerous failures. Blighted by a heightened attachment on the part of anyone who ever experienced the original, the repeated attempts to revive the much-loved British label Biba have met with perpetual failure. One of its revivals in 2006, with Bella Freud at the helm, failed to connect with either the press or consumers and missed the original point of the label – it was disposable fast fashion for teenagers, not a pastiche with designer prices. Once again Biba has been put to rest.

This tendency to revive old brands where possible raises questions about the future of the fashion industry and about how much room will be made for fresh names. This said, new designers are still making headway in this difficult market: Christopher Kane, Rodarte and Philip Lim (to name but a few) represent the persistence of the new in a market increasingly defined by nostalgia.

Alber Elbaz for Lanvin, Silk dress, 2005.
Fashion Museum, Bath, England
The appointment of Alber Elbaz as chief designer at Lanvin has been one of the most successful brand revivals of the 21st century. His designs reference the heritage of the house without descending into nostalgia. With this silk dress he has created a thoroughly modern look that makes reference to the dropped-waist styles for which Jeanne Lanvin was renowned in the 1920s.

Tom Ford for Gucci, Suit, 1996–7.
The Costume Institute, Metropolitan
Museum of Art, New York, US
As much a clever marketeer as a designer, Tom Ford successfully revived the fortunes of Italian heritage house Gucci in the 1990s and provided a template that has been copied many times since: take an established name, install a young designer who is willing to plough his or her own furrow and develop a collection and campaign that makes it relevant to the contemporary fashion market.

OTHER COLLECTIONS
FRANCE Musée de la Mode et du Textile, Louvre, Paris
ITALY Galleria del Costume, Palazzo Pitti, Florence
NORTHERN IRELAND Ulster Museum, Belfast
US Arizona Costume Institute, Phoenix Art Museum, Phoenix, Arizona; Los Angeles County Museum of Art, Los Angeles, California

Yuppieism; Postmodernism;
Celebrity Consumerism

Ritualism; Surrealism;
Utility

Vintage

 Traditionally associated with the needy and the counter-cultural, the image of second-hand clothing underwent something of a transformation towards the end of the 1990s when it became part of mainstream fashion and acquired a new name: Vintage.

 KENI VALENTI (1958–); KIRA JOLLIFFE (1972–); BAY GARNETT (1973–); KATE MOSS (1974–); CAMERON SILVER (1969–)

mainstream appropriation; individuality; connoisseurship; *Cheap Date*; archives

The emergence of Vintage as a credible alternative to 'new clothing'

in the mid- to late 1990s was part of a broader trend that emphasised the rejection of (supposedly homogeneous) mainstream fashion and encouraged individual expression through one's attire (customisation, for example, was a concurrent trend). To wear Vintage was to mark oneself out as a connoisseur and fashion individualist.

This idea was reinforced by the fashion media. Glossy magazines (usually the preserve of new and expensive fashion) extolled the joys of Vintage; a proliferation of specialist guide books offered advice on where, what and how to shop for and wear Vintage; a specialist magazine, *Cheap Date*, launched by fashion insiders Bay Garnett

and Kira Jolliffe, was an irreverent and hip take on thrift-store culture; and further endorsement came from the most important of modern-day fashion bellwethers, the celebrity. Kate Moss in particular has been a key catalyst in the widespread adoption of Vintage and Vintage-inspired trends into the mainstream and her eponymous range for high-street store Topshop is based on iconic elements of her own Vintage wardrobe.

A sanitised (and expensive) version of the Vintage experience caters to consumers more used to shopping in designer boutiques and unwilling to get their hands dirty or spend their time sifting through tat for a bargain. Decades, owned by former cabaret artist Cameron Silver, in Los Angeles caters to the Hollywood fraternity; Didier Ludot in Paris is the home of Vintage Haute Couture; and Keni Valenti, once a fashion designer himself, has become New York's self-styled 'King of Vintage'.

Keen to capitalise on a burgeoning trend, established retailers incorporated Vintage within their otherwise traditional outlets. On the high street, Topshop Oxford Street has a dedicated Vintage department and in 2008 offered Internet customers a limited range of cherry-picked garments from iconic 1960s and 1970s boutique designers. In addition, department stores such as Liberty of London and Au Printemps in Paris have areas devoted to high-end Vintage, and even charity shops have separated the more desirable garments from the run of the mill.

Although fashion has always displayed a tendency towards nostalgia, and the revival of old styles has been a constant in fashion history, the success of Vintage has impacted upon the design process and output of many major fashion houses. Taking advantage of the cachet of their own iconic heritage, some designers raid in-house archives and reproduce 'classic' pieces; in recent years, Yves Saint Laurent and Balenciaga have launched collections based on this premise. The use of specialised Vintage outlets (such as Saratoga Trunk in Glasgow and Twentieth Century Vintage Fashion in Devon) as a source of 'inspiration' for designers has also become a legitimate part of the fashion process and visits to Vintage trade fairs are as much a part of the fashion calendar as the twice-yearly prêt-à-porter shows or the textile trade exhibitions.

← **Decades Inc, Vintage gowns, store interior, Melrose Avenue, Los Angeles, California, US**
Founded in 1997 by Cameron Silver, the Los Angeles couture Vintage store Decades Inc, which holds an unparalleled stock of immaculate couture garments such as the Chanel and Nina Ricci ones on display here, has transformed the image of Vintage clothing in Hollywood and has been the source of some of the most photographed (and copied) Vintage gowns worn on the red carpet in recent years.

OTHER COLLECTIONS
By virtue of their purpose as repositories for historical dress, museums are full of garments that could theoretically be categorised as Vintage. However, these outfits should not be viewed as such. Vintage clothing is defined by its patterns of consumption and consequently it has not been possible to provide a list of museums to visit for this category. Instead, a selection of well-established and respected purveyors of Vintage clothing has been detailed, all of which are open to the public.
ENGLAND Virginia Antiques, 98 Portland Road, London
FRANCE Didier Ludot, Galerie de Montpensier, Jardin du Palais Royal, Paris
US Keni Valenti Retro Couture, West 29th Street, New York; Resurrection, Mott Street, New York

 Brand Revivalism; Nostalgic Romanticism; Postmodernism; Celebrity Consumerism

 Ritualism; Modernism; Deconstructionism

The Death of Couture

The strictly governed and elitist Parisian Haute-Couture industry was formally founded in 1864 by Charles Frederick Worth. In 1939 there were 70 members, but today only 11 remain, nearly all of which operate at a financial loss. These statistics suggest the imminent demise of what was once the most influential sector of the fashion industry. However, to paraphrase Mark Twain, reports of the Death of Couture have been greatly exaggerated and it has continued to play an important, if diminished, role in the global fashion economy.

VALENTINO GARAVANI (1932–);
YVES SAINT LAURENT (1936–2008);
JOHN GALLIANO (1960–)

Chambre Syndicale de la Haute Couture; diversification; licensing; brand identity; House of Lesage

Haute Couture literally means high sewing or high dressmaking. It is the elite sector of the fashion industry and is defined by its craftsmanship and made-to-measure ethos. Admittance to the world of Haute Couture is strictly governed by the Chambre Syndicale de la Haute Couture, which stipulates that each member must: produce two

collections per year; produce 50 new and original designs of day and evening wear for each collection; design made-to-measure for private clients with at least one or more fittings; and employ a minimum of 20 people full-time in their own Paris-based workshop. In addition to this, everything must be made in-house, by hand.

However, what was once a flourishing and vital sector of the fashion economy has experienced a marked decline since the 1950s. Astronomical price tags, a competitive and diverse market and the strict guidelines to which couturiers must adhere meant that by 2009 there were only 11 officially registered houses with four second-ranking correspondent (or foreign) members. Further, the retirement from Haute Couture of Yves Saint Laurent in 2002, followed by Versace in 2003, Emanuel Ungaro in 2004 and Valentino in 2008 compounded what has become a persistent concern among fashion commentators: Haute Couture is facing an imminent death.

← John Galliano, Evening dress for Christian Dior Spring/Summer Collection, 1998. The Costume Institute, Metropolitan Museum of Art, New York, US

John Galliano's appointment as Chief Designer at the house of Christian Dior in 1997 has helped to reinvigorate Paris couture. This lavish and romantic evening dress of black silk taffeta demonstrates his theatricality, romantic aesthetic and attention to historical detail.

The Death of Couture

These concerns are not new. In 1964, UK magazine *Queen* published a mock obituary of the Haute-Couture houses of Balenciaga and Givenchy, indicating that rapid developments in youth-driven fashion rendered this dowdy, antiquated and prohibitively expensive industry of no relevance to the modern woman. Certainly fashion was becoming pluralistic and could no longer be dictated by the elite, but the couture industry evolved appropriately and drew upon a tradition of economic tenacity that had allowed it to survive other cultural upheavals.

Designers diversified their product range and thus their source of income. No longer were they dependent on the dwindling and unprofitable Haute-Couture market. Ready-to-wear collections and the licensing of designers' names for use on perfume, eyewear, stockings and scarves have allowed companies to preserve their Haute-Couture business and enhance brand identity while lending a patina of glamour to a number of pedestrian and affordable products.

However, it is overly reductive to view Haute Couture as an elaborate marketing tool. It is responsible for the preservation and promotion of crafts and techniques that would die out were it not for the patronage of the couture houses and the supply of skilled technicians from the Chambre Syndicale couture school. These attendant industries include featherwork, glove making, millinery, ribbon making, embroidery (most notably by the House of Lesage) and button making. Most importantly though, there is still a tangible, albeit limited, market for Haute Couture, thus ensuring its future as a vital sector of the global fashion industry.

← Boudicca dress, 2006. The Museum at the Fashion Institute of Technology, New York, US
As the number of couture houses dwindled without obvious sign of newcomers to replace them, the Chambre Syndicale had to find new ways of bolstering the Haute-Couture schedule. In 2007 a number of design houses were invited to become guest participants at Haute-Couture fashion week in Paris. Boudicca, the avant-garde label by London design duo Zowie Broach and Brian Kirkby, was the first

OTHER COLLECTIONS
AUSTRALIA Powerhouse Museum, Sydney
AUSTRIA Wien Museum, Vienna
ENGLAND Victoria and Albert Museum, London
FRANCE Musée de la Mode et du Textile, Louvre, Paris
SPAIN Museo del Traje, Madrid

The New Look; The Birth of Haute Couture

Rationalism; Modernism; Mass Productionsim; Utility

Globalism is an economic, political and cultural phenomenon. As one of the most powerful industries in the world, fashion has acted as both a catalyst for the phenomenon as well as the physical expression of its development.

PHILIP KNIGHT (1938–);
DRIES VAN NOTEN (1958–);
MATTHEW WILLIAMSON (1971–)

World Trade Organization; competitive; cultural imperialism; multinational; homogenisation

The term Globalism denotes the dissolution of old nation-state boundaries to create a global economy and culture. Theoretically, we are now citizens of the world. This has been enabled by the dismantling of global trade boundaries (supervised by the World Trade Organization since 1995) and has been catalysed by the development of multicultural societies, increased travel opportunities and seismic shifts in our worldwide communication networks, most notably in the advent of the Internet, globally published magazines and internationally available television programmes.

The unceasing demand for cheap clothing and the unquenchable appetite for novelty in fashion has stimulated the worldwide development of a highly competitive and inventive manufacturing and distribution system. Fashion companies have increasingly moved their sites of production to capitalise on lower manufacturing costs. Although this strengthens the global economy and arguably brings commercial opportunity to developing countries, critics note that the itinerant tendencies of

the powerful fashion companies inhibits true global development. There is an intrinsic imbalance of power whereby the maturation of nascent economies is dependent upon the patronage of the powerful and usually Western fashion companies. Jobs are marginalised, and in an ever increasing need to keep costs down the working conditions under which many are forced to operate are compromised.

The effects of Globalism are also evidenced in the consumption of fashion. Products and brands are no longer site specific and it is a truism that multinational clothing brands (and their copies) are now available on an unprecedented level. Should one wish to purchase Nike trainers, a Marc Jacobs Stam handbag or a Lacoste polo shirt, availability is not restricted by location. This has led to complaints that local cultures are being replaced by a homogenised, Western-dominated aesthetic that represents a form of cultural imperialism. This view is problematic, though, in that it assumes the veneration of these brands and the blind susceptibility of non-Western cultures to the might of the multinationals. In truth garments are adopted and incorporated in a way that is unique to each culture.

Globalism has also accelerated the 400-year-old tendency in the West to incorporate indigenous clothing into high fashion. In 2007 British designer Matthew Williamson (who bases his collections on the 'idea of a modern girl who is a global traveller') was criticised by an official in the Ethiopian Intellectual Property office for incorporating traditional Ethiopian dress into his Spring/Summer 2008 collection.

Dries Van Noten, Ensemble, 2007,
The Museum at the Fashion Institute
of Technology, New York, US
The Belgian designer Dries Van Noten is a graduate of the Antwerp Royal Academy of Fine Arts and his work is a refined, poetic and singular take on global fashion cultures, which he incorporates into his collections in a subtle and considered manner.

Nike leather cricket boots, 1995.
Powerhouse Museum, Sydney, Australia
Nike, founded in 1964 by Phil Knight, has become one of the most successful and recognisable sportswear brands in the world. For many, it has also become emblematic of all that is wrong with Globalism. However, it has also been argued that the outsourcing of Nike's manufacturing to developing countries (such as to Indonesia where these cricket boots were produced) has in fact benefited the individual worker who is privy to better rates of pay and conditions than other workers in the local economy. What is certain is that any benefits are not the result of altruism on the part of Nike, but instead are a fortunate by-product of the never-ending search for cheaper manufacturing costs.

OTHER COLLECTIONS
BELGIUM Mode Museum, Antwerp
ENGLAND Fashion Museum, Bath;
Victoria and Albert Museum, London
JAPAN Kobe Fashion Museum, Kobe
NORTHERN IRELAND Ulster Museum, Belfast
SPAIN Museo del Traje, Madrid
US Los Angeles County Museum of Art,
Los Angeles, California

 Exoticism; Orientalism;
The Internet

 The Birth of Haute Couture;
Aestheticism; Arts and Crafts

5

REFERENCE
SECTION

Glossary of Names

A

ADAM ANT (Stuart Goddard) (1954–)
New Romanticism

ADRIAN, Gilbert (1903–59)
Hollywoodism

ALAIA, Azzedine (1940–)
Celebrity Consumerism

ALBINI, Walter (1941–83)
Return to Classics

ANTHONY, Susan B (1820–1906)
Bloomerism

ARMANI, Giorgio (1934–)
Yuppieism

ASHBEE, Charles Robert (1863–1942)
Arts and Crafts

AMIES, Hardy (1909–2003)
Utility; The New Look

ASHLEY, Laura (1925–85)
Nostalgic Romanticism

ASTAIRE, Fred (1899–1987)
Hollywoodism

B

BAKST, Leon (1866–1924)
Orientalism

BALENCIAGA, Cristobal (1895–1972)
Victorian Revivalism;
The New Look

BALMAIN, Pierre (1914–82)
The New Look

BANKS, Jeff (1943–)
British Boutique Movement

BANTON, Travis (1894–1958)
Hollywoodism

BARDOT, Brigitte (1934–)
Existentialism

BATES, John (1938–)
British Boutique Movement

BEATON, Cecil (1904–80)
Victorian Revivalism; New
Edwardianism; Existentialism

BECKHAM, David (1975–)
Football Casualism

BEENE, Geoffrey (1924–2004)
Return to Classics

BEER, Gustav (dates unknown)
Empire Revivalism

BERTIN, Rose (1747–1813)
The Birth of Haute Couture

BEST, George (1946–2005)
Football Casualism

BINGENHEIMER, Rodney (1946–)
Glam

BIKKEMBERGS, Dirk (1959–)
Deconstructionism

BIRTWELL, Celia (1941–)
Nostalgic Romanticism

BLAHNIK, Manolo (1942 –)
Celebrity Consumerism

BLOOMER, Amelia Jenks (1818–94)
Bloomerism

BOATENG, Ozwald (1968–)
Savile Row

BOLAN, Marc (1947–77)
Glam

BONNARD, Camille (dates unknown)
Pre-Raphaelitism

BORG, Björn (1956–)
Football Casualism

BOWES-LYON, Elizabeth (1900–2002)
Victorian Revivalism

BOWIE, Angie (1949–)
Glam

BOWIE, David (1947–)
Glam; New Romanticism; Football Casualism

BRETON, André (1896–1966)
Surrealism

BROACH, Zowie (dates unknown)
The Death of Couture

BRUMMELL, George Bryan 'Beau' (1778–1840)
Dandyism; Savile Row

BUBBLE, SUSIE (Susanna Lau) (1984–)
The Internet

BURNE JONES, Edward (1833–98)
Pre-Raphaelitism

BYRON, Lord George Gordon (1788–1824)
Romanticism

C

CADY STANTON, Elizabeth (1815–1902)
Bloomerism

CALLOT, Josephine, Marie, Marthe and Regina (dates unknown)
Empire Revivalism

CARDIN, Pierre (1922–)
Space Ageism

CARR, Mrs Joseph Comyns (1850–1927)
Aestheticism

CASTELBAJAC, Jean-Charles de (1949–)
Surrealism

CHALAYAN, Hussein (1970–)
Deconstructionism

CHANEL, Gabrielle 'Coco' (1883–1971)
Modernism

CHARLES II (1630–85)
Restorationism

CHILDERS, Leee Black (1945–)
Glam

CHOO, Jimmy (1961–)
Celebrity Consumerism

CLARK, Raymond 'Ossie' (1942–96)
British Boutique Movement;
Nostalgic Romanticism

COBAIN, Kurt (1967–94)
Grunge

COCTEAU, Jean (1889–1963)
Surrealism

COOK, Paul (1956–)
Punk

COOPER, John Paul (1869–1933)
Arts and Crafts

COUNTY, Jayne (1947–)
Glam

COURRÈGES, André (1923–)
Space Ageism

CRAWFORD, Joan (1905–77)
Hollywoodism

CREED, Oliver (1599–1658)
Restorationism

CROMWELL, Oliver (1599–1658)
Restorationism

CURTISS, Jackie (1947–85)
Punk

D

DALÍ, Salvador (1904–89)
Surrealism

DALTON, Hugh (1887–1962)
Utility

DASSLER, Adolf ('Adi')
(1900–78)
Football Casualism

DAVID, Jacques-Louis
(1748–1825)
Revolutionism; Neoclassicism

DE CASTELBAJAC, Jean-Charles
(1949–)
Surrealism

DE FONTANGES, Angélique
(1661–81)
Baroque

DE HAVILLAND, Terry (1938–)
Glam

DELAUNAY, Sonia (1885–1979)
Modernism

DEMEULEMEESTER, Ann
(1959–)
Deconstructionism

DE POMPADOUR, Madame
(1721–64)
Rococo; Exoticism

DIAGHILEV, Serge (1872–1929)
Orientalism

DIOR, Christian (1905–1957)
The New Look

DOUCET, Jacques (1853–1929)
Empire Revivalism

DUFF GORDON, Lucille, Lady
(1863–1935)
Belle Epoque

DUFY, Raoul (1877–1953)
Orientalism

DU MAURIER, George
(1834–96)
Aestheticism

E

EDWARD VII (1841–1910)
Belle Epoque

EGAN, Rusty (1957–)
New Romanticism

ELBAZ, Alber (1961–)
Brand Revivalism

EMANUEL, David (1952–)
New Romanticism

EMANUEL, Elizabeth (1953–)
New Romanticism

ESTEREL, Jacques (1918–74)
Existentialism

EUGÉNIE, Empress (1826–1920)
The Birth of Haute Couture

EVELYN, John (1620–1706)
Restorationism

F

FATH, Jacques (1912–54)
The New Look

FERRY, Bryan (1945–)
Glam

FISHER, Alexander (1864–1936)
Arts and Crafts

FOALE, Marion (1939–)
British Boutique Movement

FORD, Tom (1961–)
Brand Revivalism

FORTUNY, Mario (1871–1949)
Orientalism

FREUD, Bella (1961–)
Brand Revivalism

G

GABRIEL, Alfred Guillaume,
Count D'Orsay (1801–52)
Dandyism

GALLIANO, John (1960–)
The Death of Couture

GARAVANI, Valentino (1932–)
The Death of Couture

GARNETT, Bay (1973–)
Vintage

GAULTIER, Jean Paul (1952–)
Death of Couture

GERNREICH, Rudi (1922–85)
British Boutique Movement

GEORGE VI (1895–1952)
Victorian Revivalism

GEORGE, PRINCE OF WALES
(1762–1830)
Dandyism

GHESQUIÈRE, Nicolas (1971–)
Brand Revivalism

GIBB, Bill (1943–88)
World Clothing

GIBSON, Charles Dana
(1867–1944)
Belle Epoque

GIGLI, Romeo (1950–)
Minimalism

GIVENCHY, Hubert de (1927–)
The New Look

GOLDWYN, Samuel (1879–1974)
Hollywoodism

GRÉCO, Juliette (1927–)
Existentialism

GREEN, Philip (1952–)
Globalism

GREENE, Alexander Plunkett
(1932–90)
British Boutique Movement

GRÈS, Alix (1899–1993)
Modernism

GUCCI, Guccio (1881–1953)
Brand Revivalism

GUILD, Shirin (1946–)
Minimalism

H

HALSTON FROWICK, Roy
(1932–90)
Return to Classics

HARBERTON, Viscountess
(1843–1911)
Rationalism

HARTNELL, Norman (1901–79)
Victorian Revivalism;
Utility

HAWEIS, Mary Eliza (1848–98)
Pre-Raphaelitism

HEAD, Edith (1897–1981)
Hollywoodism

HEPBURN, Audrey (1929–93)
Existentialism

HOFFMANN, Josef (1870–1956)
Arts and Crafts

HORSTING, Viktor (1969–)
Deconstructionism

HOWE, Elias (1819–67)
Industrialism

HULANICKI, Barbara (1936–)
British Boutique
Movement

HUNT, Walter (1796–1859)
Industrialism

HURLEY, Elizabeth (1965–)
Celebrity Consumerism

I

IRIBE, Paul (1883–1935)
Empire Revivalism

J

JACOBS, Marc (1964–)
Grunge

JAEGER, Dr Gustav (1832–1917)
Rationalism

JAMES, Richard (dates unknown)
Savile Row

JOLLIFFE, Kira (1972–)
Vintage

JONES, Steve (1955–)
Punk

JORDAN (Pamela Rook) (1955–)
Punk

K

KANE, Christopher (1982–)
Brand Revivalism

KARAN, Donna (1948–)
Yuppieism; Minimalism

KAWAKUBO, Rei (1942–)
Japanese Avant-Gardeism

KELLY, Orry (1897–1964)
Hollywoodism

KING, Emily M (dates unknown)
Rationalism

KING, Jessie M (1875–1949)
Arts and Crafts

KIRKBY, Brian (dates unknown)
The Death of Couture

KLEIN, Calvin (1942–)
Return to Classics; Yuppieism;
Grunge; Minimalism

KNIGHT, Philip (1938–)
Globalism

L

LACROIX, Christian (1951–)
The Death of Couture

LAGERFELD, Karl (1938–)
Postmodernism

LANG, Helmut (1956–)
Minimalism

LANVIN, Jeanne (1867–1946)
Hollywoodism

LAUREN, Ralph (1939–)
Nostalgic Romanticism;
Yuppieism

LE BRUN, Elisabeth Louise Vigée
(1755–1842)
Naturalism

LIBERTY, Arthur Lasenby
(1843–1917)
Pre-Raphaelitism; Aestheticism

LIM, Philip (1973–)
Brand Revivalism

LOUBOUTIN, Christian (1963–)
Celebrity Consumerism

LOUIS XIV (1638–1715)
Restorationism;
Baroque

LOUIS XV (1710–74)
Rococo

LOUIS XVI (1754–93)
Revolutionism

LOVE, Courtney (1964–)
Grunge

LUDOT, Didier (dates unknown)
Vintage

M

MacINNES, Colin (1914–76)
Existentialism

McCARDELL, Claire (1905–58)
Modernism

McCARTNEY, Stella (1971–)
Celebrity Consumerism;
The Death of Couture

McGOWAN, Cathy (1943–)
Celebrity Consumerism

McLAREN, Malcolm (1946–)
Punk; New Romanticism

McQUEEN, Alexander (1969–)
The Death of Couture

MARGIELA, Martin (1957–)
Deconstructionism

MARIE ANTOINETTE (1755–93)
Naturalism;
Revolutionism

MASSENET, Natalie (1965–)
The Internet

MATLOCK, Glen (1956–)
Punk

MEISEL, Steven (1954–)
Grunge

MILLAIS, John Everett (1829–96)
Pre-Raphaelitism

MIYAKE, Issey (1938–)
Japanese Avant-Gardeism

MOLYNEUX, Edward
(1891–1974)
Utility; The New Look

MOORE, Bobby (1941–93)
Football Casualism

MOORE, Mandy (1984–)
Celebrity Consumerism

MORI, Hanae (1926–)
Japanese Avant-Gardeism

MORRIS, Jane (1839–1914)
Pre-Raphaelitism

MORRIS, William (1834–96)
Arts and Crafts

MORTON, Digby (1906–83)
Utility

MOSCHINO, Franco (1950–94)
Surrealism;
Postmodernism

MOSS, Kate (1974–)
Grunge; Vintage

MUGLER, Thierry (1948–)
Yuppieism

MUIR, Jean (1928–95)
Return to Classics

N

NEWBERY, Jessie (1864–1948)
Arts and Crafts

NUTTER, Tommy (1943–92)
Savile Row

O

OBERKAMPF, Christophe-
Philippe (1738–1815)
Exoticism

O'DOWD, (Boy) George (1961–)
New Romanticism

O'NEILL, Olive (dates unknown)
Mass Productionism

OLSEN, Ashley and Mary-Kate
(1986–)
Celebrity Consumerism

OSTI, Massimo (1946–2005)
Football Casualism

OWENS, Rick (1962–)
Deconstructionism

P

PAQUIN, Jeanne (1869–1936)
Empire Revivalism

PARKER, Sarah Jessica (1965–)
Celebrity Consumerism

PARKINSON, Norman (1913–90)
New Edwardianism

PATOU, Jean (1880–1936)
Modernism;
Victorian Revivalism

PEPYS, Samuel (1633–1703)
Restorationism

PERKINS, Sir William Henry
(1838–1907)
Industrialism

PLUNKETT, Walter (1902–82)
Victorian Revivalism

POIRET, Paul (1879–1944)
Empire Revivalism; Orientalism

POOLE, Henry (1814–76)
Savile Row

POP, IGGY (James Osterberg)
(1947–)
Glam

PORTER, Thea (1927–2000)
World Clothing

PRADA, Miuccia (1949–)
Brand Revivalism

PRINCE ALBERT (1819–61)
Ritualism

PUCCI, Emilio (1914–92)
Brand Revivalism

Q

QUANT, Mary (1934–)
British Boutique Movement

QUEEN ALEXANDRA
(1824–1925)
Belle Epoque

QUEEN VICTORIA (1819–1901)
Ritualism

R

RABANNE, Paco (1934–)
Space Ageism

REAGAN, Ronald (1911–2004)
Yuppieism

RÉCAMIER, Madame
(1777–1849)
Neoclassicism; Empire Revivalism

RHODES, Zandra (1940–)
Nostalgic Romanticism;
Punk

RICCI, Nina (1883–1970)
The New Look;
Brand Revivalism

RITTER, Lou (dates unknown)
Mass Productionism

ROBERTSON, Nick (1968–)
The Internet

ROBESPIERRE, Maximilien
(1758–94)
Revolutionism

ROGER, Neil Munro 'Bunny'
(1911–97)
New Edwardianism

ROSSETTI, Dante Gabriel
(1828–82)
Pre-Raphaelitism

ROTH, Christian Francis (1969–)
Grunge

ROTTEN, Johnny (John Lydon)
(1956–)
Punk

ROUSSEAU, Jean-Jacques
(1712–78)
Naturalism

RUSKIN, John (1819–1900)
Arts and Crafts

RYKIEL, Sonia (1930–)
Return to Classics

S

SAINT LAURENT, Yves
(1936–2008)
Existentialism; World Clothing;
Return to Classics; The Death of
Couture

SANDER, Jil (1943–)
Minimalism

SCHIAPARELLI, Elsa (1890–1973)
Surrealism; Victorian Revivalism

SCHUMAN, Scott (1968–)
The Internet

SCOTT, Sir Walter (1771–1832)
Romanticism

SHAW, George Bernard
(1856–1950)
Rationalism

SHELLEY, Mary (1797–1851)
Romanticism

SHEPHERDSON, Jane (1963–)
Globalism

SILVER, Cameron (1969–)
Vintage

SIMONS, Raf (1968–)
Deconstructionism; Brand
Revivalism

SINGER, Isaac Merritt (1811–75)
Industrialism

SIOUX, Siouxsie (Susan Ballion)
(1957–)
Punk

SMITH MILLER, Elizabeth
(1822–1911)
Bloomerism

SNOEREN, Rolf (1969–)
Deconstructionism

SNOW, Carmel (1887–1961)
The New Look

SOO CATWOMAN (Soo Lucas)
(1955–)
Punk

SPENCER, Earl (1758–1834)
Neoclassicism

SPENCER, Lady Diana (1961–97)
New Romanticism

STARKE, Frederick (1904–88)
Mass Productionism

STEPHEN, John (1934–2004)
British Boutique Movement

STIEBEL, Victor (1907–76)
Utility

STRANGE, Steve (Steven
Harrington) (1959–)
New Romanticism

SUI, Anna (1964–)
Grunge

T

TAKADA, Kenzo (1939–)
Japanese Avant-Gardeism

THATCHER, Margaret (1925–)
Yuppieism

THEYSKENS, Oliver (1977–)
Brand Revivalism

TUFFIN, Sally (1938–)
British Boutique Movement

U

UNGARO, Emanuel (1933–)
Space Ageism; The Death of
Couture

V

VALENTI, Keni (1958–)
Vintage

VAN BIERENDONCK, Walter
(1957–)
Deconstructionism

VAN NOTEN, Dries (1958–)
Deconstructionism; Globalism

VERSACE, Donatella (1955–)
Celebrity Consumerism

VERSACE, Gianni (1946–97)
Celebrity Consumerism

VICIOUS, Sid (Simon Ritchie)
(1957–79)
Punk

VIONNET, Madeleine
(1876–1975)
Modernism

VIVIER, Roger (1913–98)
The New Look

W

WARD, Mary Augusta
(1851–1920)
Aestheticism

WARHOL, Andy (1928–87)
Punk

WATANABE, Junya (1961–)
Japanese Avant-Gardeism

WATTEAU, Jean-Antoine
(1684–1721)
Baroque

WATTS, GF (1817–1904)
Pre-Raphaelitism

WESTWOOD, Vivienne (1941–)
Punk; New Romanticism

WILDE, Oscar (1854–1900)
Dandyism; Aestheticism

WILDE, Constance (1858–98)
Aestheticism

WILLIAMSON, Matthew (1971–)
Globalism

WINTERHALTER, Franz Xavier
(1805–73)
Victorian Revivalism

WOLFE, Tom (1931–)
Dandyism

WORTH, Charles Frederick
(1826–95)
The Birth of Haute Couture

WORTH, Gaston (1853–1924)
The Birth of Haute Couture

Y

YAMAMOTO, Kansai (1944–)
Glam

YAMAMOTO, Yohji (1943–)
Japanese Avant-Gardeism

A

ATELIER
The studio or workshop of a Haute-Couture designer.

ANILINE DYE
An artificial dye derived from indigo, invented in 1856 by Sir William Perkin. Colours were bolder than those extracted from the traditional animal and vegetable dyes.

ARTIFICIAL SILK
Term used to describe rayon fabrics in the late 19th and early 20th centuries.

B

BANYAN
An indoor dressing gown for men popular during the 17th and 18th centuries. Named after a cast of Hindi merchants banyans were traditionally made from Indian linen, but became more common in silks, wool and cotton. A status symbol, gentlemen had their portraits painted while wearing them.

BESPOKE
A garment that is made individually to a person's specific requirements from scratch. Said to have originated in Savile Row in the 17th century; when tailors held a length of cloth for a particular customer it was said to 'be spoken for'. Not to be confused with made-to-measure clothing which is fashioned from an existing template and then adjusted to individual requirements.

BIAS CUT
Cloth that is cut diagonally across the grain, allowing it to stretch and follow the contours of the body. The technique was perfected by Madeleine Vionnet and became particularly fashionable in the 1930s.

BLOOMER
Loose, short pantaloon trouser usually gathered at the knee.

BRICOLAGE
The practice of adopting and recombining diverse and existing styles to create a new whole.

BROCADE
A heavy fabric woven on a jacquard loom to create a complex raised pattern.

BUSTLE
Padding or a cage used to create volume to the rear of a skirt below waist level. Bustles were popular in the latter half of the 19th century.

C

CANNONS
In menswear, bunches of ribbon or a lace frill worn at the knee for decorative purposes.

CHAMBRE SYNDICALE DE LA HAUTE COUTURE
The governing body of the Paris Haute-Couture system. Founded by Charles Frederick Worth in 1868 it monitors member houses to ensure they are complying with the strict regulations that allow them to be defined as Haute-Couture houses.

CHINOISERIE
European interpretation of a 'Chinese' style. Not usually based upon first-hand experience but assumptions and sometimes prejudices.

CLOCHE
A bell-shaped, form-fitting hat usually made from felt that was popular during the 1920s.

CORSET
A form-fitting undergarment stiffened with whalebone, metal or wood and tightened with lacing. It was named during, and came to define the silhouette of, the 1800s, though it had been popular for some time. In the 18th century, corsets were known as 'stays' in England and 'corps à baleines' in France.

CRINOLINE
From the French *crin* (horsehair), and *lin* (linen), the crinoline was originally a full petticoat made from these woven fabrics. The caged crinoline was developed in the 1850s and enabled the extraordinarily wide silhouette popular in the mid-19th century.

COUTURE
A broad term that literally translates as sewing or dressmaking. Usually refers to made-to-measure clothing of an exceptional standard. Often mistakenly used to describe Haute Couture and vice versa.

D

DJELLABAH
A North African hooded cloak with wide sleeves.

DRAPER
A merchant of cloth and other sewing paraphernalia.

E

EMPIRE LINE
A high-waisted style where the seam is placed directly under the bust. It was named after and popularised by Empress Josephine during the French Napoleonic Empire (1804–14).

F

FICHU
A small triangular scarf or shawl used to hide the décolletage that was popular in late 18th and early 19th centuries.

FRENCH CUFF
Otherwise known as double cuffs, these fold back on themselves and are fastened with a cufflink. Found on a male shirt and traditionally viewed as a formal style.

FROCK COAT
Adapted from a military style, a knee-length coat with tails, collar and sometimes a full skirt (hence the name). Frock coats became formal wear for men in the early part of the 19th century.

G

GARCONNE
A boyish, flat-chested and tubular silhouette for women extremely popular during the 1920s.

GIGOT (LEG O' MUTTON SLEEVES)
Sleeve full from the shoulder and tapered to the elbow and wrist. The volume of the top of the sleeve varies according to prevalent fashions.

GROSGRAIN
A closely woven and heavily ribbed fabric. Made originally from silk, it was used for ribbon and trimmings.

H

HAUTE COUTURE
The strictly governed, Paris-based elite sector of the fashion industry. Admittance to the world of Haute Couture is

governed by the Chambre Syndicale de la Haute Couture which stipulates strict rules that members must obey. Often mistakenly used to describe Couture and vice versa.

HOBBLE SKIRT
A skirt cut full and then narrow towards the hem which allowed the wearer to take only very small steps. Hobble skirts were introduced by Paul Poiret and were popular before the First World War.

J

JABOT
A cascading ruffle of lace, embroidery or a sheer fabric that is attached to the front of a dress or outfit at the neck.

JULIETTE SLEEVE
A long, fitted sleeve with a puff at the shoulder.

K

KAFTAN
A long tunic with a slit neck and wide sleeves that originated in North Africa and the Middle East. Kaftans found popularity as home- or holiday wear in the late 1960s and 1970s.

L

LYONS
Centre of the French silk industry from the 18th century.

M

MARCHANDE DE MODE
A supplier of trimmings who exerted huge influence upon

fashion until the 19th century. The most famous was Rose Bertin who became chief fashion adviser to Marie Antoinette.

MUSLIN
A plain, woven, usually cotton fabric made in various weights. It was first imported to Europe from Mosul (Iraq) in the 17th century and then manufactured in England and France.

N

NYLON
Introduced in 1939 by American chemical company DuPont, nylon is a generic name for a synthetic fibre composed of a long chain of polyamides.

P

PANIER
Hoops or a basket-like structure worn on the hips and underneath skirts to create volume. Paniers were fashionable from the 1720s until the French Revolution of 1789.

PETER PAN COLLAR
A small, flat and round-tipped collar.

PRINCESS LINE
A fitted silhouette without waist seams that was fashionable from the mid-1860s and was popularised by Charles Frederick Worth.

R

REDINGOTE
Based on the English riding coat originally worn by men in the 18th century, the redingote evolved to become a woman's long-sleeved gown with

matching coat in the early 19th century.

READY-TO-WEAR (PRÊT-À-PORTER)
Clothing made by a designer that is not made to measure and is bought off the peg.

S

SMOCK
A loose-fitting garment.

SMOCKING
A panel of material tightly gathered with decorative stitching.

SUMPTUARY LAW
Restriction placed upon the ownership of luxury goods and garments to particular social groups or classes.

T

TOILE
A prototype garment made in a cheap fabric by a designer to test its design and construction.

TULLE
A fine-gauze fabric of hexagonal mesh. It was originally made of silk, but in the 20th century often made from nylon.

U

ULTRASUEDE
A synthetic, crease-resistant, machine-washable fabric that mimics the feel of suede and became particularly fashionable in the 1970s.

W

WATTEAU
A sack-back dress style popular in the early 1700s, so called because they are captured in the paintings of Jean-Antoine Watteau.

WARP
Threads that run lengthways and are interwoven with the weft.

WEFT
Threads that run crosswise and are interwoven with the warp.

WHALEBONE
From the upper part of the whale's jaw, used to stiffen corsets and crinolines. Whalebone became so popular in the mid-1800s that the whale was threatened with extinction.

Z

ZIP
Patented in 1893 and developed through the first years of the 20th century, the zip was originally used for tobacco pouches and money belts and then was adopted by the US Navy to fasten their windproof jackets. The earliest designer to use and make ao feature of this item was Elsa Schiaparelli.

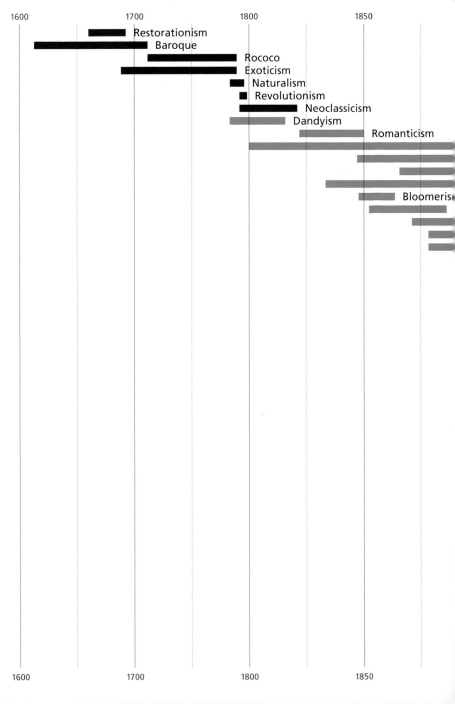

Restorationism
Baroque
Rococo
Exoticism
Naturalism
Revolutionism
Neoclassicism
Dandyism
Romanticism
Bloomeris

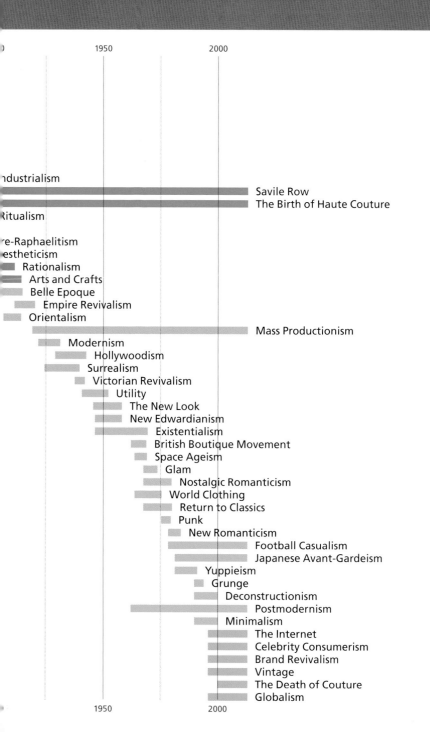

1950　　　　2000

Industrialism
Savile Row
The Birth of Haute Couture
Ritualism
Pre-Raphaelitism
Aestheticism
Rationalism
Arts and Crafts
Belle Epoque
Empire Revivalism
Orientalism
Mass Productionism
Modernism
Hollywoodism
Surrealism
Victorian Revivalism
Utility
The New Look
New Edwardianism
Existentialism
British Boutique Movement
Space Ageism
Glam
Nostalgic Romanticism
World Clothing
Return to Classics
Punk
New Romanticism
Football Casualism
Japanese Avant-Gardeism
Yuppieism
Grunge
Deconstructionism
Postmodernism
Minimalism
The Internet
Celebrity Consumerism
Brand Revivalism
Vintage
The Death of Couture
Globalism

1950　　　　2000

AUSTRALIA
Melbourne National Gallery of Victoria; **Sydney** Powerhouse Museum

AUSTRIA
Vienna Austrian Museum of Applied Arts; Kunsthistorisches Museum; Modesammlung des Historischen Museums; Wien Museum

BELGIUM
Antwerp Mode Museum; **Hasselt** Modemuseum

CANADA
Montreal McCord Museum of Canadian History; **Toronto** Textile Museum of Canada; **Winnipeg** Costume Museum of Canada

CHILE
Santiago Museo de la Moda

CHINA
Nantong Nantong Textile Museum

CZECH REPUBLIC
Prague Museum of Decorative Arts

ENGLAND
Bath Fashion Museum; **Birmingham** Birmingham Museum and Art Gallery; **Bradford** Bradford Industrial Museum; **Brighton** Brighton Museum and Art Gallery; **Bristol** Bristol City Museum and Art Gallery; **Exeter** National Trust, Killerton House; **Guildford** Watts Gallery, Compton; **Hull** Ferens Art Gallery; **Liverpool** Walker Art Gallery; **London** Geffrye Museum; Imperial War Museum; Museum of Childhood; Museum of London; National Portrait Gallery; Tate Britain; Victoria and Albert Museum; The William Morris Gallery; **Manchester** Gallery of Costume, Platt Hall; **Nottingham** Abington Park Museum; **Walsall** Walsall Museum; **Warrington** Warrington Museum and Art Gallery; **Whitby** Whitby Literary and Philosophical Society; **Worthing** Worthing Museum and Art Gallery; **York** York Castle Museum

FINLAND
Helsinki Finnish National Gallery; **Jyväskylä** Craft Museum of Finland

FRANCE
Avallon Museum of Costume; **Lyons** Musée des Tissus et des Arts décoratifs; **Paris** Musée de la Mode et du Costume de la Ville de Paris, Palais Galliéra; Musée de la Mode et du Textile, Louvre; **Versailles** Museum of French History

GERMANY
Darmstadt Institut Mathildenhöhe; **Hamburg** Museum für Kunst und Gewerbe; **Munich** Bavarian National Museum

HUNGARY
Budapest Museum of Applied Arts; **Gödöllo** Gödöllo Municipal Museum

INDIA
Ahmedabad The Calico Museum of Textiles

ITALY
Florence Galleria del Costume, Palazzo Pitti; **Venice** Fortuny Museum, Museo Civice di Venezia

JAPAN
Kobe Kobe Fashion Museum; **Kyoto** Kyoto Costume Institute; **Nara** Nara National Museum

THE NETHERLANDS
Utrecht Centraal Museum

NORTHERN IRELAND
Belfast Ulster Museum; **Magherafelt** National Trust, Springhill, The Lenox-Conyngham Collection

PORTUGAL
Lisbon Museu Nacional do Traje e da Moda,

REPUBLIC OF SOUTH AFRICA
Johannesburg Bernberg Museum of Costume

RUSSIA
St Petersburg State Hermitage Museum

SCOTLAND
Aberdeen Aberdeen Art Gallery and Museum; **Dumfries** National Museum of Costume, Shambellie House; **Edinburgh** National Museum of Scotland; **Glasgow** Hunterian Museum and Art Gallery

SPAIN
Guetaria Fundación Balenciaga; **Madrid** Museo del Traje

SWEDEN
Stockholm Moderna Museet; Nationalmuseum; Nordic Museum

US
Boston Museum of Fine Arts; **Chicago** Chicago History Museum; **Cleveland** Rock and Roll Hall of Fame and Museum; **Columbus** Ohio State University Historic Costume and Textiles Collection; **Indianapolis** Indiana State Museum; **Los Angeles** The Fashion Institute of Design and Merchandising; Los Angeles County Museum of Art; **Madison** State Historical Society of Wisconsin; Wisconsin Historical Museum; **New York** The Bard Graduate Center for Studies in the Decorative Arts, Design, and Culture; Brooklyn Museum; Cornell Costume and Textile Collection, Cornell University, Ithaca; The Costume Institute, Metropolitan Museum of Art; The Museum at the Fashion Institute of Technology; Museum of the City of New York; **Orlando** Hard Rock Cafe; **Philadelphia** Drexel Historic Costume Collection, Drexel University; Philadelphia Museum of Art; **Phoenix** Arizona Costume Institute, Phoenix Art Museum; **Providence** Museum of Art, Rhode Island School of Design; **Seattle** Experience Music Project, Science Fiction Museum and Hall of Fame; **Seneca Falls** Seneca Falls Historical Society Archive Collection; **Washington DC** National Museum of American History, Smithsonian Institution; Textile Museum

WALES
Powys Llanidloes Museum; Newtown Textile Museum; Powysland Museum, Welshpool

First published in the United States
of America in 2010 by
UNIVERSE PUBLISHING
A Division of Rizzoli International
Publications, Inc.
300 Park Avenue South
New York, NY 10010
www.rizzoliusa.com

AN IQON BOOK
This book was designed
and produced by
Iqon Editions Limited
Sheridan House
112–116a Western Road
Hove BN3 1DD

Publisher, concept and direction:
David Breuer

Designer: Isambard Thomas

Editor and Picture Researcher:
Caroline Ellerby

Printed in Singapore by
Star Standard

ISBN: 978-0-7893-1826-8

Library of Congress Control
Number: 2009930800

2010 2011 2012 2013 /
10 9 8 7 6 5 4 3 2 1

**Cover Illustration details
(left to right, from top):**

Terry de Havilland, Platform shoe,
1972. Walker Art Gallery (p. 98)

Cecil Beaton, Audrey Hepburn
dressed in black, 1954. National
Portrait Gallery, London (p. 92)

Tom Ford for Gucci, Suit, 1996–7.
The Costume Institute,
Metropolitan Museum of Art
(p. 135)

Muslin gown and shawl, 1800–11.
Victoria and Albert Museum (p. 28)

Back detail of taffeta bodice and
skirt, c 1869. Victoria and Albert
Museum (p. 40)

Paul Poiret, 'Sorbet' evening dress,
1912. Victoria and Albert Museum
(p. 70)

Oswald Boateng, Suit, 1996.
Victoria and Albert Museum (p. 43)

Biba woman's gold lamé jacket,
1965–9. Victoria and Albert
Museum (p. 99)

Paco Rabanne, Chain-linked dress,
1967. Museo del Traje (p. 97)

Yves Saint Laurent, Evening dress,
1967. The Museum at the Fashion
Institute of Technology (p. 103)

Gianni Versace, Evening dress,
Spring/Summer 1001. The Costume
Institute, Metropolitan Museum of
Art (p. 133)

Louis Vuitton, 'Speedy' travelling
bag, 2001. Powerhouse Museum
(p. 129)

Gentleman's suit with matching
cape, 1670s. Victoria and Albert
Museum (p. 14)

Painted Chinese silk polonaise
dress, c 1770. The Costume
Institute, Metropolitan Museum of
Art (p. 22)

Silk brocade robe à la française,
c1760. Kyoto Costume Institute
(p. 19)